PENGUIN

HOW TO
BE A GENIUS

$$Z_o = \frac{138}{\sqrt{E_r}} \log\left(\frac{D}{d}\right) (ohms)$$

$$f_e = \frac{11.8}{\pi\left(\frac{D+d}{}\right)\sqrt{}}$$

HOW TO
BE A GENIUS

PAUL BARKER

PENGUIN BOOKS

CONTENTS

About the author

Test results suggest that Paul Barker could be a bona fide genius, though he does appear to have been 'on the cusp' for a while. He has successfully* pursued careers in a variety of fields (see Why I Am Not a Genius) and was specifically* chosen to write this book because of his polymathic knowledge, his commitment to the genius self-help movement, and his ability to knock out a thousand words in three and a half hours. He is currently, as mathematicians say, 'working on some problems'.

How to use this book

The best way to use this book is to read it. The best way to read it is to dismantle it, taking care to save the cover and the binding, and then to paste the pages in numerical order across one wall of your living room. Once you have done this you should set yourself a daily reading target and stick to it. The publishers cannot be held responsible for the consequences of any reader's failure to stick to a reading schedule. Any reader's principle aim should be to think about what he or she reads. Always.

(*Adverbs may not be accurate)

So You Want to Be a Genius?

'One is not born a genius, one becomes a genius.'

SIMONE DE BEAUVOIR

SO YOU WANT TO BE A GENIUS?

YOU WANT TO BE A GENIUS. GOOD FOR YOU. YOU COULD ALREADY BE OVER THREE-FIFTHS OF THE WAY THERE. YOU COULD BE STANDING ON THE BRINK OF FAME, FORTUNE, ALL SORTS OF OTHER BRINKS. TEST THE WATERS.

A taste for the genius life

'Put your talent into your work, but your genius into your life.' – Oscar Wilde

Who wouldn't want to be a genius? Geniuses inspire awe. They extend humanity itself. They are history's elite. They shake things up. Geniuses have outstanding and unique talents that are intellectual and often creative in some sense. (A world-beating songbird impersonator is unlikely to be recognised as a genius. Not unless he or she does something else besides.) In layman's terms, the genius thinks something new. That's what inspires the awe.

As well as deification in your field, if you're a genius, you can expect to enjoy:

- Rich and powerful people liking you*

- People hanging on your every word

- Becoming more sexually attractive

- Winning prizes on a regular basis

- Sycophants paying your bills

* Although it must be said that some might dislike you in equal measure.

Common misconceptions

There are a number of widely held ideas about genius that are just plain wrong. (If you are a genius you will obviously be able to identify and dispel these flawed ideas.) Football players are not geniuses. Golfers are not geniuses either. These truths, though self-evident, are painful for some. But they shouldn't be. The fact is geniuses love truth. They crave it. Pain and all.

Culture is relative, accumulative, and tricky. It's tempting to see sports personalities, actors, singers and film directors as geniuses, privileging us with new emotional and psychological experiences that we didn't know we could have. But it's safer just to see them as entertainers. Entertainers can be geniuses (see chapter four), but it's rare. Geniuses from the arts need to be considered using measures of universality, longevity and formal development. It is complicated (unless you're a genius).

Other common misconceptions

- That it's all one per cent inspiration, ninety-nine per cent perspiration. The greater the first percentage, the smaller the second. That's the way percentages work.

- That you have to wear a robe

- That you cannot be bald

- That you are not human

- That you have to be completely nuts

LEONARDO DA VINCI (1452–1519) – POLYMATH

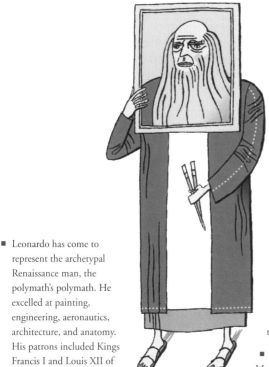

- Leonardo has come to represent the archetypal Renaissance man, the polymath's polymath. He excelled at painting, engineering, aeronautics, architecture, and anatomy. His patrons included Kings Francis I and Louis XII of France, Giuliano de' Medici and Cesare Borgia.

- Among other things, he invented the helicopter over four centuries before anyone got around to building one.

- His contribution to his teacher Andrea del Verrocchio's painting The Baptism of Christ marks the beginning of the Italian High Renaissance.

- He often wrote his notes in mirror writing. This may have been an attempt to keep his ideas top secret, or a method he devised as a left-hander to avoid smudging the ink.

- In 1504 he painted the Mona Lisa, a likeness most probably of the wife of Francesco del Giacondo, which would become the world's most famous portrait.

- Leonardo's superstar status makes him a favourite of conspiracy theorists: he's been accused of everything from faking the Turin shroud to concealing the bloodline of Christ.

Have you got what it takes?

> 'Talent, lying in the understanding, is often inherited;
> genius, being the action of reason or imagination, rarely
> or never.' – Samuel Taylor Coleridge

Obviously an outstanding talent is only the first requisite. It guarantees nothing. You also need stamina, grit, luck, not to die of consumption before puberty – things like that. But if you pretend those things don't count, or you can find an analytical system that allows you to discount or at least suspend their influence, then you can get yourself a checklist and start ticking boxes. Even geniuses enjoy that.

Your potential

Use these eleven steps – the test is an IQ test in that it is an Interesting Questionnaire – to assess how easy or unlikely it will be for you to become a genius. Note that this questionnaire should only be used by people over the age of four, unless in extreme genius circumstances.

Could you be a genius?

1. Do you like . . . ?
    a) Maths
    b) Physics
    c) More maths and more physics
    Score one point for a) and/or b). Two points for c).

2. Are you interested in . . . ?
    a) The universe
    b) Universals
    c) Golf
    One point for b), two points for a). Odd, really.

3. As a child, did you watch . . . ?
    a) Cartoons
    b) Russian cinema of World War II
    c) The cat
    Three points for c), two for b). It just about makes
    sense if you think it through.

4. Have you ever . . . ?
    a) Found a four-leaf clover
    b) Designed a cathedral
    c) Registered an invention
    Two points for more than one of any of the above.

5. Have you ever said . . . ?
    a) 'Knowledge is the precarious peak upon

which we stand to survey the world.'

b) 'Knowledge is the library and stuff. Right?'

c) 'No ledges on my windows.'

The correct answer is none of the above. Two points.

6. Rate the following statements on a scale of one to ten, one being, 'no way!' and ten being, 'I'm the boss, I'm the boss, I'm the boss!'
   a) 'I would sacrifice my wife, my children, my home – everything for my career.'
   b) 'All I need to do is take Crowthorne's thesis out of Professor Lodge's pigeonhole and replace it with my own.'
   c) 'I really, really like maths.'

   If you rate any of the statements at more than five, your potential just won another two points.

7. Which are you, generally . . . ?
   a) Yes
   b) No
   c) Maybe

   Not surprisingly, 'no' gets nothing. Otherwise, bag the numbers: one for a), two for c).

8. You feel most comfortable in:
   a) The lab
   b) A dusty university study
   c) A franchised coffee bar

   Owing to contractual obligations, a) and b) get you two points, c) gets you four. And remember, genius loves a cappuccino to go!

9. The previous eight questions have been patronising and have failed to engage my intellect.
   a) Agree
   b) Disagree
   c) Feel emptiness and ennui
   No points for disagreeing. Otherwise, help yourself.

10. Which statement comes closest to tinkering with your brain waves?
    a) 'Physical exercise helps me focus my thinking.'
    b) 'Physical exercise makes me look fit and thus more attractive to the opposite sex.'
    c) 'Physical exercise? No way!'
    A point for each one. Potentially three points.

11. Final thoughts?
    a) OK
    b) Yep
    c) Cappuccino?
    Yes, c) gets the points.

So, check your score. Lots of points is good. Not many is bad. And anything in between is, well . . . in between.

As a genius, you should, by now, have realised that the questionnaire is as meaningless as meaningless can be. It is merely a way of making you think about your own life and its potential for genius.

Methods for improving your
brain power

You've got potential. You're on your way. But an outstanding intellect, like any muscle, requires regular exercise. You need to get yourself some strategies that keep your brilliant mind at its brightest and best. That dazzling brain of yours needs constant polishing.

The following tips are some tried-and-true methods for getting your cognitive cogs a-turning. Using them can only do you good.

- Whenever making a cash transaction, try to work out the change in your head before the cash register does.

- Whenever you are walking along an urban street, try to estimate the number of parked cars and the length of the street. You will be able to calculate the average space taken up by each vehicle and you can work out the street's maximum parking capacity. You could decide on a minimum distance necessary between each car and introduce that factor into the equation. Be careful not to get run over – that hampers your chances of achieving the exalted status you seek.

- Think outside boxes, envelopes, and other containers. Try to make unusual conceptual concordances. What happens if you strap a mouse to a tennis ball? What if you teach a snake to play the guitar? This helps you to develop new ideas and new inspirations. Can an electric eel power a microwave for four minutes?

- Get a notepad and write the word 'IDEAS' on the front. If you're right-handed do it with your left hand and vice versa. That way it will look childish and historians will think you had your ideas in your prodigious youth.

- Memorise things. Your super-brain needs as much information to crunch on as it can get. Feed it. (See chapter six for more on this.)

- Read complicated books. This is one of the basic strands of genius training. You need to know what everyone else has thought in order to make sure your idea is original.

- Try thinking in new ways: numbers, shapes, colours, metaphors. The ability to think differently is an important and useful skill.

AVOIDABLE BEHAVIOUR

Avoid the following traits if you are going to make the most of things.

- **Laziness.** Laziness is all right in some ways. But even if you are draped across a chaise longue, out of your mind on the finest Chinese opium, you should always be mentally focused on your current project.

- **Stupidity.** There is no way around it – genius is not stupid. If you find yourself being stupid, snap out of it by thinking something complex.

- **Ideological Commitment.** If you nail your colours to a mast, you may find your ship sinking. A genius believes in the truth. That's all there is.

- **Addiction.** A genius is almost as vulnerable to addiction as regular folk. All those potential geniuses that never made it because addiction got them – we don't even know their names.

- **Commercialism.** Do not do it for the cash. You might make lots of money, and good luck to you if you do. But it shouldn't be your motivation. It simply won't work.

- **Boredom.** After childhood, when it's OK, boredom must not be tolerated. It should function only as a fleeting reminder that things need to be done. Those with super-brains ought to use them.

- **Jokes.** Know any good philosopher jokes? Exactly.

- **Violence.** There are always exceptions. In general though, 'live by the sword, die by the sword' is a tad extreme for your average particle physicist.

- **Hobbies.** Once you're world-renowned, get a train set by all means. Aspiring geniuses don't have the time.

CHAPTER ONE

The Pros and Cons of a Genius Lifestyle

'Innovators and men of genius have almost
always been regarded as fools at the
beginning (and very often at the end)
of their careers.'

FYODOR DOSTOYEVSKY

THE PROS AND CONS
OF A GENIUS LIFESTYLE

BEING A GENIUS SERIOUSLY AFFECTS YOUR LIFE. INDEED, IT BECOMES YOUR LIFE. SO YOU NEED TO ASSESS THE BALANCE OF ADVANTAGES AND DISADVANTAGES IF YOU'RE THINKING OF DOING SOME GENUINE BOUNDARY-PUSHING.

The fruits of genius

It might seem that being a genius is a golden ticket to a life of glamorous soirées with the intellectual elite, champagne flute in hand, arm candy at your side, surrounded by a throng of smiling sycophants. But you might be confusing this scene with the lifestyle of a diplomat. Get your expectations right from the start. First, let's consider the many advantages.

Status

Genius is the ultimate in status. You can be a great; you can be a colossus; you can be a legend. As a genius, you also have mystery. The whole point is that nobody has access to some truth about the world in the way you do. People are bound to gaze at you in awestruck amazement. This can be satisfying. Geniuses *are* godlike – above mundane human experience. Most importantly, they think the new thought for us. And this is the most precious of gifts. Newton showed everybody that the universe is like some big mechanical toy, and he had the maths to prove it. He got to be Master of the Mint and President of the Royal Society. Yes, the genius's gift changes the world for us. So they get R-E-S-P-E-C-T.

Social space

What can you do with respect? For the godlike intellect, there is available a whole impressionist's palette of exclusion from social regulations. You certainly shouldn't feel you need to behave or appear as an ordinary mortal would.

Fashion statement

Pianist Glenn Gould was always worried about being cold. Even when it wasn't cold. So he wore big overcoats and hats when he gave concerts. Einstein sometimes didn't wear socks. You can exclude yourself from convention because you have higher concerns. And it's OK.

'I'm with the genius'

When it comes to behaviour, knock yourself out! The situation is helped by other people's expectations and allowances. 'He's Bertrand Russell, I had to sleep with him!' sounds like a reasonable sentiment. The same can be said for, 'Of course he twitches as though he had no control over his body. He's Samuel Johnson, the inventor of the dictionary!'

Make a name for yourself

Get your name attached to something. The Pythagorean theorem, or the Möbius strip – something catchy like that. Ideally, you should be looking for a neat, universal law to be named after you. You may not be familiar with *On the Electrodynamics of Moving Bodies*, but you've probably heard of $E=mc^2$. You may be vaguely aware that a body immersed in a fluid is buoyed up by a force equal to the weight of the displaced fluid, but you're more likely to have heard of Archimedes's principle.

The genius's name becomes synonymous with his or her ideas – consider Darwin, Newton, Curie. Yes, the genius's *name*. Because that's what will live forever – your name and your idea, of course, but not you. It's a *kind* of living forever. But not one that you can experience. And anyway, what is 'forever'?

With any luck you could get a decade or two of solid fame and adulation. This should make it worth the effort. Everyone knows who you are, you can put your sartorial and social inadequacy plans into action, and you can really live the life of the super-being.

Feel-good factor

Then, of course, there's that good old-fashioned smug self-satisfaction. That idea you had – your dazzling thought – you were right! And now the whole world sees the whole world in a different light, a light that shines your name upon the heavens. Or, maybe the world just gets to see triangles from a fresh perspective; the point's the same. Humanity's understanding of the many mysteries of its own experience has moved one step further along the long highway of enlightenment. Thanks to you. Give yourself a pat on the back. Everyone else is doing it.

ISAAC NEWTON (1642–1727)
– PHYSICIST, ASTRONOMER, MATHEMATICIAN

- The son of a Lincolnshire, English, farmer, Newton went to Trinity College Cambridge. He went on to become a fellow there and was made a professor in 1669.

- Interested in optics – to the extent that he once stuck a spike in his eye socket to see what would happen – Newton invented the reflecting telescope, a vast improvement on the existing single-lens telescope.

- His genius work, Philosophiae Naturalis Principia Mathematica, was published in 1687. It introduced the laws of motion and universal gravity.

- There were problems of attribution for Newton, and he became involved in a dispute with Gottfried Leibniz over the discovery of differential calculus. According to their peers, they both invented it simultaneously.

- Knighted by Queen Anne in 1705 (for his work at the Royal Mint rather than any scientific achievement), Newton was deservedly buried in Westminster Abbey.

- Poet Alexander Pope treated Newton's legacy with greater respect. He composed the famous epitaph: 'Nature and nature's laws lay hid in night / God said, "Let Newton be" and all was light'.

But now the down side . . .

If the advantages haven't put you off, consider the disadvantages. The whole of this chapter is one great big elastic equation. In a way.

Prepare to be a loner

The genius lifestyle often involves a lot of time spent alone. This is because of the thinking time required and the practicalities of writing the play or the opera or the calculations. Not only is it lonely at the top, it's lonely on the way there too. You will have to shun friends, destroy enemies, develop a ruthless streak.

Cut off from social interaction, your quest to formulate your ideas may consume and destroy you; your brilliance may fade into silence. Philosopher Immanuel Kant seemed not to have thought anything for at least a decade in the late 1700s and it looked for a while as though he had lost it. But he came back strongly with the dazzlingly clever *Critique of Pure Reason* and sealed his reputation. If you can take the knock to your social life, the isolation will pay off in the end.

There ain't no sanity clause

Genius can make you go mad. The reason is what's technically called 'brain burn'. This is a condition that can affect geniuses from time to time. Usually it goes away with a bit of bed rest or some electric shock therapy or trepanning. If they do zap the juice out of you and you're already established as a genius, they won't want to keep you and you'll be able to go home and blabber like an imbecile there. That's the happier option.

And sometimes your genius itself can be downright depressing. You may not have discovered a wacky new chemical that everyone finds amusing; you may have revealed an unpalatable truth about our lives or our world. Your genius might be to discover exactly how our world is about to meet its imminent doom. Don't expect your research project to be a barrel of laughs.

You mean he was a genius after all?

To be avoided at all costs is posthumous recognition. Depending on your point of view, this is either really bad luck or the gods taking it out on you with a vengeance.

Often it's not quite so severe – if you're a Shakespeare or a Mozart or a Caravaggio, you do get plenty of recognition during your lifetime. It's just that your contemporaries, clever though they obviously must be, might not appreciate just how special your talent is. You could, however, end up in the poorhouse, or out of favour, lonely, bankrupt and forced to sell all your stuff like Rembrandt. The bottom line is that you may end your life not knowing if posterity will bestow its blessing.

Be optimistic, though. You know you're right. They'll realise in time.

Cultivate the genius lifestyle

Test the boundaries of style slowly: egg on your tie one week, sweater on backwards the next. But try to be original. Too many people just go for lab coat and trainers. Bor-ing.

1. Whatever your style decisions, remember to wash. No one wants to bestow a Nobel Prize on a smelly scruff.
2. Be modest in the presence of presidents and kings – they're just not clever enough to understand why you're greater than they are.
3. Make sure your name sticks to the idea. This is best achieved by staying alive as long as possible. Had Charles Darwin fallen under a bus before he published, the name Alfred Russel Wallace would undoubtedly be attached to the idea of natural selection today.
4. The journey from isolated study to brightly lit social whirl can be quick and startling. But do try to remember the important names – princes, presidents, prime ministers, popes.
5. Your genius may well attract power. Be careful. For the artistic or scientific genius, politics is a dangerous arena. You may know more physics than anyone alive, but politicians don't play by rules.
6. If you want to use your ideas to make money, don't be afraid to be a self-publicist. It doesn't hurt Stephen Hawking's profile to appear on *The Simpsons*.
7. If you are an artistic genius, hang on to the money. You will, of course, make a comeback, but you might not be alive to see it.
8. Make sure you go out sometimes. A brisk walk is good for you.
9. Finally, all the other tips are eclipsed by 'the idea'. Pursue 'the idea' at all costs.

A SUMMARY OF THE PROS/CONS

The public will adore and worship you unfalteringly.	Your peers will resent and undermine you. Unfalteringly.
People always think of you when they draw triangles. You reveal a fundamental truth. About triangles.	People know nothing about you, except that once you said something about triangles.
You can behave as though you are totally crazy.	Your fundamental truth is not popular.
You can behave as though you are totally and completely crazy.	You might actually be totally and completely mad.
Your name lives forever and stretches into eternity.	You do not actually get to live forever. Much as you may want to.

CHAPTER TWO

Early Signs of Genius

———◆———

'The reluctance to put away childish things
may be a requirement of genius.'

REBECCA PEPPER SINKLER

EARLY SIGNS OF GENIUS

NOT ONE HUNDRED PER CENT SURE YOU ACTUALLY ARE A GENIUS? THERE ARE SIGNS. STUDY THEM. YOU SHOULD AT LEAST BE GOOD AT THAT SORT OF THING — INTERPRETING AND SUCHLIKE.

The prodigy and the slow starter

Lots of geniuses have been prodigies. So prodigious behaviour is definitely something to look for. Some good questions to ask yourself: How many operas have I written? Did I stand in the library with my hands at my sides discoursing with the university lecturers from my father's college when I was only six? Were my teenage years spent in the shed making gadgets and explosions? Is my dad away laying siege to Byzantium? If your answers are five, yes, yes and yes, respectively, you're already close.

Another excellent indicator of the early promise of great greatness is the 'astounding feat'. The astounding feat is something that sets the prodigy apart from his or her peers. This might be something like publishing a novel or writing a symphony while still in your teens, but a good sign generally is surpassing the abilities of your teachers.

If you're not a prodigy you needn't worry, you can still be a genius. In fact, even if you majored in mediocrity until your thirties, if you really lay claim to the title with a world-shaking idea or invention, biographers will mythologise your past until it turns out that you had been able, after all, to recite pi to 50 decimal points when you were only four. But it helps if you give them some material to work with.

WOLFGANG AMADEUS MOZART (1756–1791) – COMPOSER

- The son of Leopold, deputy Kapellmeister to the court orchestra of the Archbishop of Salzburg, Mozart made his first professional European tour aged six.

- The 'Amadeus' part of his name is the Latinised version of one of the names that appears on his birth certificate: Theophilis.

- In 1782 he married Constanze Weber against the wishes of his father. She was a good wife and bore him six children, but she couldn't manage her husband's spending. Mozart was in debt when he died and was buried in a communal grave in Vienna.

- Joseph Haydn was one of Mozart's close friends. Haydn called him the greatest composer he knew. The two played music together and were even members of the same lodge of Freemasons. Mozart's opera *Die Zauberflöte* (*The Magic Flute*) is said to contain Masonic symbols and ideas.

- Mozart wrote 15 masses, more than 50 symphonies, 21 piano concertos and 21 stage or operatic works.

- Two popular myths, fed by Peter Shaffer's play and subsequent film, *Amadeus*, are that Mozart was poisoned by his colleague Antonio Salieri, and that he felt that he was writing his final requiem for himself, rather than Count Walsegg, the man who commissioned it.

What it means if you love equations

You're eight years old. It's a Sunday and it's raining. You are watching the raindrops streaking down the outside of the windows. Something occurs to you about the number of streaks and the speeds at which they run. You see an idea in your mind – not in words or symbols, but in shapes and absences – that makes you feel that the idea has some fundamental truth. You realise soon afterwards that mathematical ideas slot simply into your mind, and the relationships between them seem immediately clear. You are thinking about complicated ideas and it makes you feel good. You are on your way.

Fostering good obsession

Thinking about complicated ideas is something that geniuses have in common and do a lot. When most people think about complicated things they get a headache or get angry or drunk. The fact that your fizzy imagination enjoys complexity gives you an edge. This pleasure, while helpful in keeping you hardworking and dogged, can edge itself into obsession. One risk with which the genius frequently struggles is that his or her field of excellence will become an escape from real life, with all its vicissitudes. Clinically, there are two kinds of obsession: good obsession and bad obsession. Good obsession keeps you motivated and curious; bad obsession destroys you and those around you. The choice may or may not be yours.

Falling in love with quadratics

To most people algebra and equations are boring things that maths teachers make you do in order to ruin your teenage years. But then it lies beyond most people to understand the unfailing gorgeousness of an equals sign, the jaunty knowingness of brackets, or the universal mystery that is x^2. These algebraic icons give the youthful maths prodigy a way of seeing the world as meaningful and balanced. Equations are not only examples of sparkling perfection in a world chock-full of ugliness and decay; they also last. So if you are a budding numbers genius, look for a snappy equation to help your name endure.

Eccentricity as standard

One of the best things about being a genius is that people expect, and therefore are more prepared to tolerate, a certain eccentricity of behaviour. You can deliver lectures wearing your slippers, become catatonic during a dinner party, be socially incompetent, or even go nuts. Experiment.

Your great mind has a different way of seeing and the great masses know this. Often the more batty behaviour you exhibit, the more adulation you'll receive. As a genius, you're like a seer, or perhaps a shaman. Your role is to act as if there is a higher knowledge, another reality. Which, of course, there is. Your genius reassures the masses of exactly that fact.

Keeping out of a straitjacket

There is, however, a downside to the bonanza of quirky tics that is you. The man in the street also half-expects that your weird lifestyle might, at times, necessitate the odd spell in a straitjacket, holed up in the padded suite of a gothic Victorian asylum. Your wackiness might be interpreted in the light of the idea that there is a thin line between genius and madness. And you may, on reflection, find that you actually are mad. In which case you shouldn't be too surprised by the odd spell in the bouncy dungeon. The problem is that your thinking has to border on the edges of reason, and hanging out on the borders of reason takes its toll.

Part of your social inadequacy may stem from your over-treading the path of the solitary individual. The hours of free-associating and zapping neural connections while walking in the lonely hills above the town make you a stranger to the rules of conversational dynamics and liable to be too spontaneous, blurting out something painfully immature or petulant. Take into account, though, that lots and lots of people are strangers to the rules of conversational dynamics and are forever blurting out some nonsense. So don't worry too much. Social frigidity or flammability is really only part of a larger scheme of very odd behaviour.

Think of a way to be eccentric and endearing. That's the most popular combination. It can be as easy as always wearing the same dilapidated cardigan every day or calling everybody 'mysterious bard'. It seems like a little thing, but biographers love this kind of individual touch.

FIVE WAYS TO REACH ECCENTRIC BEHAVIOUR

- Spend as much time as you can thinking
- Say everything that comes into your head
- Keep notes on everything
- Hardly ever finish anything
- Spend as much time as possible alone

Who's your daddy?

Parentage is often important for the genius. Essentially you should be looking for something a little bit different. Perhaps your father was a noble and your mother a peasant girl. Perhaps you had a gypsy uncle who would play the violin at family events and encouraged your love of anthropology. Perhaps you were raised at court and personally tutored by a Greek philosopher. All are good signs and bode well.

Your loss is your gain

There are some general points to factor in when considering your childhood. It helps if your parents are emotionally flawed or absent or alcoholic or dead. You need something to give you an early sense of loss or grief or yearning. If your mother dies in childbirth or your father dies before you're born, that helps too.

Like it or not, some good psychological scarring will pay dividends in the long run. The mechanism by which these dividends will be realised is that the youthful prodigy enters a world of emotional and intellectual loneliness and isolation. (According to most health professionals, loneliness and isolation should be taken only in moderation, but short bursts can free the imagination from the interference of things like friendships, romances, and that old chestnut: the dead hand of social conformity.)

Being a loner does, of course, have risks. Some loners do not in fact become geniuses – they become psychopaths. Psychopathology should be discouraged.

Family structure? An adoptee, an orphan, an only child, one of 12, over-loved by the father, neglected by the father, neglected by both parents, neglected by both parents and all of your 11 siblings (until that one day at breakfast, on your 10th birthday, when you spoke and they all suddenly realised). Whatever the scenario, it doesn't matter much. Any family combination has possibility. As ever, isolation and some form of childhood neglect or trauma usually helps.

School is overrated

Unless you're being apprenticed to a Florentine painter, school is often not that important. Being educated at home and alone by a brilliant parent or some pedagogic guardian can accelerate the learning process, thus giving you intellectual superiority over your childhood peers (should you meet any) and encouraging you to think that life is about hard work. It should also ensure that you have problems socialising. Remember that whether they're strapping you to a violin at the age of four or farming you out to a crazy aunt for your formative years, your folks are just doing their bit to help you along Genius Avenue.

The genius gender

Throughout human history women have risen to the top when allowed. It's the 'when allowed' bit that's been the *problème femme* in the genius world rankings. If we look, we can see plentiful evidence of female achievement. Consider the work of Sofonisba Anguissola (court painter for Philip II, remember?), or the brilliance of a Clara Peeters still life (which I'm sure you've seen at least once on a postcard).

Long odds

Too often patriarchal cultures have forbidden or discouraged the participation of women. Just look at the case of Clara Schumann: pianist, composer, and wife of Robert Schumann. In fact, let Clara speak for herself. One minute she's like, 'There is nothing that surpasses the joy of creation', and then she's all like, 'A woman must not desire to compose'. If you are a woman and considering the path of genius, you will need extra reserves of determination to weather the rainy Monday morning of patronising assumptions and sexist bigotry*.

The odds against a man becoming a genius are 1:238 million. The odds against a woman becoming a genius are 1: 812 million. As Pythagoras once said, 'Do the maths'.

---

* Another possible route for aspiring women is known as the 'power behind the throne' scenario. It's sort of genius by proxy. You will need a powerful and intelligent man lacking in imagination. A buyers' market.

Your hidden pedigree

The following background checklist will allow you to assess the promising mulch of your developmental years. It should be interpreted metaphorically, symbolically, and loosely. Look for the good in people, including yourself, and excepting professional rivals.

Are you a genius in the making?

1. You have a degree from:
   a) The Sorbonne
   b) The Academy at Athens
   c) The Internet

2. Your hobby is:
   a) Playing Internet chess against a super-computer
   b) Composing verse epics using a language that you invented
   c) Playstation

3. At your birth, the midwife said:
   a) 'A boy!'
   b) 'What is that?'
   c) 'Oh, it's a girl. Never mind, Mrs Einstein.'

4. Your childhood best friend was:
    a) Imaginary
    b) Your mother
    c) Douglas from next door

5. Your favourite music is:
    a) A quintet for strings that you wrote when you were 12
    b) John Cage's silence thing
    c) Abba

6. Your father says things like:
    a) 'The pope has summoned me to Rome.'
    b) 'You are a beam of light, my child, a beam of light.'
    c) 'I didn't get laundry detergent because it wasn't on the list.'

7. Your guinea pig was called:
    a) Euclid
    b) x^2
    c) Mister Guinea Pig

8. Your earliest ambition was to be:
    a) A train driver
    b) Immortal
    c) Driving a BMW by the age of 21

If you scored mostly a)s or b)s, you might be genius material. If you got mostly c)s, focus on developing your eccentric side to compensate. It's your only chance.

TOP FIVE JUNIOR ACHIEVERS

- **Wolfgang Amadeus Mozart.** Dad-tutored, little Wolfie was a precocious tot. A veteran performer by the age of eight, he was always bound for greatness.

- **Blaise Pascal.** Dad-tutored, and frequently surrounded by philosophers, he was a sure thing to start dashing off treatises in his teens.

- **Pablo Picasso.** Dad-tutored, a veritable painting infant, he was never really destined to finish school.

- **Leonardo da Vinci.** At least Da Vinci was farmed out by his dad. But again, the teenage apprentice soon outshines his master.

- **William Sidis.** Aged 11, he delivered a talk on 'four-dimensional bodies' to the bigwigs at the Harvard Mathematical Club. Always a bit shy, he became something of a recluse.

CHAPTER THREE

A Brief History of Genius

'If you would understand anything, observe
its beginning and its development.'

ARISTOTLE

A BRIEF HISTORY OF GENIUS

AS AN ADVANCED APE, YOU ARE A PRODUCT OF YOUR GENES; BUT, INTELLECTUALLY, YOU ARE A PRODUCT OF YOUR ENVIRONMENT. YOUR ENVIRONMENT NEEDS TO BE INTELLECTUALLY DYNAMIC. THIS WILL REQUIRE SOME LUCK. FOR EXAMPLE PHILOSOPHY, MATHS, CULTURE AND THINKING IN GENERAL WERE BIG WITH THE ANCIENT GREEKS, BIG WITH EARLY ISLAM, BUT NOT SO BIG WITH THE MEDIEVAL CHRISTIAN CHURCH.

The philosophy whiz kids

Want to know how it all got started? Let's take our minds back to another age. An age pre- almost everything. An age in need of something to talk about. Step up, Heraclites, Pythagoras, Socrates, Plato, Aristotle, Aeschylus, Aristophanes, Euripides, Sophocles, Homer. A top squad. They gave us philosophy, poetry, drama, some mathematics, politics – you know, 'culture'. They may have inherited some of their ideas from other civilizations, but why complicate things? What they wrote down and passed on was a conviction that proof was key to knowing stuff. Rational deduction was the way ahead. Still sounds fresh, doesn't it? It's also another magical key to the state of genius – you will need to prove it.

Socratic method

Socrates liked to ask lots of questions as a way of getting to truths. Looking for contradictions and agreements and suchlike. Hardly seems like a big deal now, but it started ethics as a field of inquiry and got philosophy in general off to a strong start.

Ask too many questions, though, and they might get fed up with you and make you drink hemlock, like what happened to poor old Socrates. Whatever your field of conceptual toil, remember that ideas can be dangerous, they can upset people and their value may go down as well as up.

The cluster

Think about it: Socrates teaches Plato. Plato sets up the Academy, the world's first philosophy department, and teaches Aristotle. Aristotle teaches some boy who later becomes Alexander the Great. OK, so Alexander didn't go into teaching, but this bunch of classical brainiacs makes a good case for the idea of an early genius hot spot in the Mediterranean.

Too busy watching gladiators

For some reason Roman philosophers just didn't do it like the Greeks. Roman philosophers did exist but they just didn't reach the peaks. Then Christianity settled in Europe and philosophy stars as Sleeping Beauty for hundreds of years. In the Middle East a brand-new religion, Islam, gives philosophy a home. Someone had to keep that learning-and-proving bug alive.

The old days are back

Thank God for the Renaissance? No, thank Aristotle and the boys from Greece and Rome, back in fashion again after more than a millennium. It's time for a whole new cornucopia of philosophers with crazy and memorable names: Copernicus, Machiavelli, Erasmus, Montaigne, Descartes, Spinoza.

And on it went, a veritable Enlightenment – Kant, Hegel, Marx, Nietzsche. A whole bucketful of world-class thinking. Philosophy, once again, laying claim to the home of genius.

The maths gurus

This time we can start with the Babylonians, the Egyptians, and the Sumerians. They sort of developed geometry. It helped with agriculture and building. But, again, it was the Greeks who picked the ball up and ran with it. In much the same way that James Brown is known as the Godfather of Soul, Euclid is known as the Godfather of Geometry for his maths book, *Elements*. Euclid got it written down so that we can read it today. Which leads to another principle of genius development: genius needs to be recorded if it is going to survive.

What's it made of?

Science, like maths, is complicated. The history of science is complicated too. Chemistry, physics, and biology do turn up in ancient history, but not in a way we would recognise. Certainly, pre-scientific cultures liked tin, lead, gold, copper and bronze, so there was a bit of basic chemistry going on. But as with geometry, a particular group of people wanted to get systematic about things. Empedocles came up with the idea that all matter is made of elements. Brilliant! But he decided they were earth, wind, fire, and water. Interesting – and popular with pagans still – but not quite so brilliant. A bit of a wild guess, really. Democritus thought that all matter was made of particles (*atomos*), which turned out to be another top-shelf idea. Even if it was not really developed for a couple of millennia.

Middle age crisis

In the Middle Ages, science is all about alchemy and gunpowder. (This trend – science as a means of making wealth or war – is, of course, still with us today.) There is a real need for genius to come along and point out that alchemy is a load of garbage. But the process is gradual. The Renaissance gives birth slowly to the Enlightenment. The process involves various be-wigged, be-ruffed, and bewildered, eccentric aristocrat-types noting that different stuff has different properties and that perhaps you could analyse and group 'elements' according to these properties. Then various wacky guys use 'experiments' to 'invent' various wacky chemicals. Hydrogen and oxygen are 'discovered'. It's all a bit chaotic and piecemeal. And a good time for geniuses.

Perhaps the biggest name in chemistry, Dmitry Mendeleyev, is so big because he finally sorted out those elements with his periodic table – named, possibly, after a kitchen table on which he periodically worked. In 1869, his table and its magic key – atomic weight – organised the elements that Empedocles had had a brainwave about all those centuries ago. Mendeleyev crosses the finish line first, winks roguishly at the crowd, and collects his genius badge.

STEPHEN HAWKING (1942–) – PHYSICIST

- Hawking started studying mathematics at University College, Oxford, before switching to physics because he thought it would be more interesting. Later, after beginning a postgraduate course in astronomy at Oxford, Hawking changed subjects and universities, deciding that theoretical cosmology at Cambridge would be more interesting.

- Amyotrophic lateral sclerosis, a form of motor neuron disease also referred to as Lou Gehrig's disease, struck Hawking when he was 21. He was given only a few years to live. Although the illness made him severely disabled, he is still alive and working.

- *A Brief History of Time* is Hawking's best-known book. First published in 1988, it has sold over nine million copies.

- In 1975, Kip Thorne from the California Institute of Technology had a bet with Hawking about the existence of black holes: If they were proved to exist, Thorne would get a year's subscription to *Penthouse*. If they were proved not to exist, Hawking would get four years' subscription to *Private Eye*. Hawking has conceded defeat.

- In a 1993 episode of *Star Trek*, Hawking appeared as himself.

The modern genius

The modern genius is exemplified by none other than Stephen Hawking. He's modern because he's computerised and techno. And yet he's also science fiction, which makes him a sort of paranormal fictional character. It's definitely a tough act to follow. You would have to do something like establish yourself as a genius and then clone yourself and then you could grow up to be another genius and so on and so forth. But you should really have realised by now that it doesn't work like that.

History test

1. According to Henry Ford, history is:
   a) Junk
   b) Drunk
   c) Bunk
   d) Funk

2. Philosophy started in:
   a) 455 B.C.E.
   b) 555 B.C.E.
   c) 2000 B.C.E.
   d) Cavemen's heads

3. The term 'renaissance' means:
   a) Re-arrangement

b) Rebirth

c) Re-design

d) Re-mortgage

4. Oscar Wilde famously told a customs officer that he had nothing to declare but his . . .

a) Genius

b) Platypus

c) Pyjama tops

d) Suitcase of booze and cigarettes

5. Phrenology is the now obsolete science of determining personality by means of:

a) A friendly questionnaire

b) Head bumps

c) Talking over a beer

d) Embalming in wax

6. Finish Karl Marx's catchphrase: 'History repeats itself, first as tragedy, second as . . . '

a) Farce

b) Slapstick

c) Documentary

d) Live album

The answers are available by reading history.

THE OLD SCHOOL

- **Socrates.** One of history's greatest and best-known philosophers, he never wrote anything down. That's confidence.

- **Plato.** A fine example to any aspiring genius, Plato's move from wrestling to political philosophy was a majestical leap of faith.

- **Aristotle.** Well travelled and influential though he may have been, Aristotle failed to notice that whales are mammals.

- **Pythagoras.** Imagine being bound for all human history to a right-angled triangle. Have some sympathy for poor Pythagoras.

- **Aeschylus.** Although virtually responsible for inventing drama as we know it, this couldn't save Aeschylus from a hideously quirky death. An eagle dropped a tortoise on his bald head, thinking it was a stone. The blow killed him.

- **Aristophanes.** This Greek showed, amazingly enough, that you can write a play called *The Frogs* and still be a genius.

- **Euripides.** In order to take drama forwards, Euripides made his plays funny and sad. In a very old-fashioned way, he was a bit modern.

- **Sophocles.** Sophocles was the top Greek playwright. He won more first prizes than anybody else. And he also gave the world, via Dr. Sigmund Freud, the ever-disturbing idea that men might desire their mothers.

- **Heraclites.** Only fragments of his work still exist, and he wrote in riddles – the perfect foundation for a lasting reputation.

- **Homer.** It may be that Homer didn't exist as a single person. He does now.

CHAPTER FOUR

Fields of Genius

———◆———

'Philosophy becomes poetry and science
imagination, in the enthusiasm of genius.'

BENJAMIN DISRAELI

FIELDS OF GENIUS

SO WHERE SHOULD YOU INVEST YOUR GARGANTUAN INTELLECT? IT'S CERTAINLY A PROBABLE CASE TO SPECULATE THAT SOME FIELDS OF UNDERSTANDING ARE BIGGER HITTERS THAN OTHERS. TRY SOME OF THESE ON FOR SIZE.

Can you prove you exist?

Philosophy makes a nice claim for being the original site of thinking new ideas. You can hear the teacher in the first lesson of your first philosophy class: 'Everything is philosophy; philosophy is everything'. (The psychology guy is saying something similar in the next classroom.)

Philosophy is odd. It's like the ultimate intellectual pursuit, yet who knows any philosophy? Who knows a philosopher? The media yell at you about the human genome project or robots on Mars, but when do they ever say anything about the current state of national philosophy? Philosophy may be in one of its periodic states of flux, presently waning a bit. Certainly not to be counted out, though.

Cold and calculating?

Again, getting your name on something is what counts – and counting may be important to you. The Pythagorean theorem may not have been the Pythagorean theorem. But it doesn't matter now. Pythagoras is the man. That's the way it goes with maths geniuses. You need something to attach to your name so you can be remembered. We know that Möbius had a strip and Pascal a triangle. Their ideas are way too complicated for most of us, so we need something that we understand. If you are a maths super-mind, get a rhombus, or a dodecahedron. Make it yours. Or else maybe you could try computing.

Baffle them

Mathematical paradoxes are a good, solid way of getting your name some currency. You don't even need to give people an idea they can use, more a problem that someone will have to resolve further down the long bumpy road of discovery. Zeno's paradoxes about motion and distance worked for him for centuries and can still get people scratching their heads today. Even greats like Aristotle and Leonardo felt the need to have a paradox. Aristotle has Aristotle's wheel paradox, which even manages a little bit of mystery.

Whatever happened to that old chemistry set?

Chemistry, a growth area in the Enlightenment, now seems a bit tired. There are, however, still openings for the ambitious genius who feels comfortable around Bunsen burners and flasks. If you're looking to be a genius in the next generation or so, chemistry looks a good bet if you've got a gold-plated, copper-bottomed solution to global warming. A solution where we all still get to stay alive.

Let's get physical

One field of inquiry where genius is currently a-happenin' is physics. Physics has produced some first-class examples. Genius is a term never uncertainly applied to Isaac Newton or Albert Einstein – two figures who walk in the truly godlike upper echelons of the G-word's spatial metaphor for hierarchy. And they are godlike because they looked over the fence at God's greenhouse – the heavens. They figured it all out with some dazzling brain work and told us that either God wasn't up there, or his plan was way crazier than anyone had thought. Big stuff.

Physics gives us the modern world, the nuclear age, the big bang, photons, electrons, quarks – all those things that we don't understand but know explain an awful lot. Physics is apparently on the lookout for a 'unified theory' that will 'explain everything'. It's there for the taking – your name attached to the explanation of everything. It would look great on your resume, get you into all sorts of exclusive parties and onto all sorts of exclusive committees.

Problem-solving

Of course, you could always solve a paradox. But only do this if you have to. Goldbach's conjecture, and the Euler-Mascheroni constant are all still available. And there's prize money up for grabs. You are, however, tying yourself to someone else's name tag, and you would do better to find your own idea.

Bodily functions

> 'Cloning may be good and it may be bad. Probably it's a
> bit of both. The question must not be greeted with reflex
> hysteria but decided quietly, soberly and on its own
> merits. We need less emotion and more thought.'
> – Richard Dawkins

If you don't fancy physics, biology is hot too. Neuroscience
and genetics, in particular. Be the first person to clone yourself.
The trouble for the potential genius here is that ethics
(welcome back, Socrates!) might become a consideration. But
then biology and medicine have always held hands in a
bloodstained way – 18th-century anatomists were known to
resort to grave robbing and even murder if the supply of corpses
dried up.

Think about the moral maze if and when you get
there. You are propelled forwards by the desire to find out.
Keep going. Let's be blunt about this genetics thing. Where is it
all heading? Eternal life, that's where. That's the public's silent
prayer (the public is here understood to mean those in the
developed world with money). So, if you and your genetics
pals down at the university labs could fix something up, what
better way to ensure your name lives forever than by actually
living forever?

A skilled hand? Join the arts

Perhaps you like to paint, write, or play the piano? You should consider being an artistic genius. As an artist you see the world in a way that other people don't, until you show them. Then they say, 'Oh yes! I see the world like that too. I just didn't realise I did'. You make the new familiar and the familiar new. A wicked illusion.

Bear in mind here that it's not necessarily the invention of something that will get you the genius tag. It could be the expertise of its use. Do we remember Filippo Brunelleschi for his work on perspective or do we remember the painters who came after – the da Vincis and Donatellos? Similarly, Shakespeare wasn't too bothered about coming up with his own stories. Thomas Kyd had already written a play called *Hamlet* when Shakespeare decided that, yes, he could probably do something with that gloomy Danish prince story.

Geniuses do homework

If brushes, palettes, and smocks are your thing, consider how history's artistic geniuses have distinguished themselves. Look at all the Renaissance greats: they tended to be apprenticed at an early age to established practitioners, whom they then outshone. Whether you're a painter or a physicist, you have to absorb a lot of stuff before you get to do the business yourself. Even Picasso got plenty of proper painting under his belt before he went all modern. His dad was an art teacher.

Play it again, Wolfgang

'Nor do I hear in my imagination the parts successively,
I hear them all at once. What a delight this is! All this
inventing, this producing, takes place in a pleasing,
lively dream.' – Wolfgang Amadeus Mozart

If you like to tinkle the keys, you might want to look to your dad as well. Bach, Mozart, and Beethoven all had heavy-duty dads, driving their progeny on to greatness. If this is currently your situation, bear in mind that your dad, as well as driving you to insanity, should be able to help you get commissions and jobs with the royal family or the pope or at least that soundtrack for the blockbuster movie. Make sure he does his bit. You're his investment too.

Bringin' it all Bach home

Ideally, your music should advance what were previously thought to be the boundaries of the possible in form and/or style. It should also somehow mystically trigger emotional responses in us that make us feel that there are human universals and that they can be felt and you can understand other people and other people can understand you and that all this is somehow significant. Or insignificant if you're in a minor key. Sounds like quite hard work, but composers and musicians are well-known debauchees and slackers, so it probably isn't.

What are words worth?

Writing is just talking written down. Being a genius at it, though, takes a bit of thought and maybe some artful borrowing from other writers. But you do have some choices here. You can always introduce a new form. Who would have thought that nobody had invented the novel until Miguel de Cervantes wrote *Don Quixote*? He saw a gap in the market, filled it with a satirical take on the values of chivalry and medieval romance told as an episodic prose narrative, and now he's wearing his genius badge with appropriate aplomb. And the reading public is saying, 'Yes, novels are what we want'.

Bard to beat

Another choice is to take complete mastery or 'mistressy' of as many forms as possible – tragedy, comedy, history, pastoral, historical-pastoral, tragic-historical, tragic-comical-historical-pastoral – and smash any professional opposition by producing the most unbelievable body of work. Think of Shakespeare's plays. (If you're wondering about the dad thing, Shakespeare's dad was no great shakes. He did get to be mayor of Stratford but he wasn't known for writing sonnets or anything.) What you write must inform and confirm. You need to show people what humanity is and what it can mean and by doing this remind them of their own humanity, of the comedy of love and the tragedy of mortality, and all that sort of stuff. What are you waiting for? Get your notepad.

Got a posse? Try leadership

Can a politician, a monarch, a soldier, or the leader of a Marxist peasant uprising really be classed as a genius? If so, how is their success to be gauged? Lands conquered and enemies slaughtered? The greatest number of live human sacrifices? The longest stretch of peacetime prosperity? The biggest army? The most polished speech?

It seems like an acceptable conversation piece to say that Alexander the Great or Genghis Khan or Erwin Rommel were military geniuses. But it probably isn't. They may have possessed outstanding intellectual ability; they may have bettered all their peers by a country mile, dying with their hands still gripping the levers of power; they may have had intense dads. But Rommel wasn't Newton, and Genghis Khan wasn't Johann Sebastian Bach. It would be a crazy world if they had been.

Alexander vs Aristotle

Let's allow some brain space for the example of Aristotle and Alexander the Great. Alexander went for the option of having power in his lifetime. And for a period of time he must have rightly boasted that he was the mightiest man in the world. Respect! But Aristotle, mere tutor to the boy king, still has his ideas taught today. Obviously, Alexander the Great does get a mention in schools, but as history – a name on the list of great men. Aristotle lives when we think about what he said.

ALEXANDER THE GREAT (356–323 BCE) – WARRIOR KING

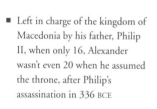

- Left in charge of the kingdom of Macedonia by his father, Philip II, when only 16, Alexander wasn't even 20 when he assumed the throne, after Philip's assassination in 336 BCE

- In his youth, Alexander was tutored by the famous Greek philosopher Aristotle.

- He conquered the Thracians, the Illyrians, the Persian Empire, and much of the then-known world. His years of campaigning took him as far east as India, where he is remembered as 'Sikander', a term used as a synonym for 'expert'.

- In 323 BCE, at the age of only 32, but battered and worn after over a decade of fighting, Alexander fell ill following a drinking bout. He died within a fortnight.

- His marriage to Roxana, daughter of Oxyartes of Bactia, was said to be because of her beauty, but it undoubtedly had political advantages as well. The same can be said of his affair with Statira, wife of Darius III – reputed to have been murdered by Roxana.

- Although he is credited with marking the beginning of the Hellenistic Age, Alexander's empire fractured soon after his death as his generals squabbled over the spoils.

Know your field

Once you have decided on a field, you need to know what has been done so that you can know what still needs to be done.

Maths and science

These should give you an almost infinite number of ideas.

- Euclid's *Elements*. Want to be big in maths? Read this book.
- Newton's *Philosophiae Naturalis Principia Mathematica*. The original manual for the universe.
- Charles Darwin's *The Origin of Species by Means of Natural Selection* is a tome for those interested in origins and species.

Art

Cast your eyes over . . .

- *Adoration of the Magi* by Leonardo da Vinci. Brilliantly unfinished.
- *Birth of Venus* by Sandro Botticelli. You've got to love the flowers.
- *Guernica* by Pablo Picasso. It's a spiky world.

Literature

Obviously the problem of language occurs. So, let's be inclusive.

- Shakespeare is nice and weighty and, of course, contains all you need to know about human nature and its expression in language.

- As a bit of a genius's genius, Johann Goethe really deserves a look. If you speak German, try his *Faust* or *Gotz von Berlichingen*.
- Naturally French needs a look as well. Give anything by Emile Zola or Gustave Flaubert or Alexandre Dumas a read. Formidable!

Music

In one sense music is an international language, in another sense it isn't. Again, inclusivity is a watchword here.

- To wrap your ears around modernity's take on what noises to make in the concert hall, try Schoenberg.
- From Dixieland to Davis, if you like jazz, you'll need to know how to improvise. Go, Cat!
- Listen to the Beatles, the Rolling Stones, Stevie Wonder. Don't listen to anything after 1979.

Philosophy

Chat these around:

- Aristotle produced something called Nichomachean Ethics. It sounds like an espionage novel. But it's so much more.
- When rationalist René Descartes wrote his *Meditations* in 1641, little did he know that 'I think therefore I am' was going to provide punning idiots with material for centuries.
- Immanuel Kant's *Critique of Pure Reason* definitely has the killer title here.

Making it your day job

As a genius, you have a reasonable-to-good chance of making some money out of your condition. But some ends are deader than others and you should at least give the money-spinning potential some thought, even if you are 'doing it for the benefit of mankind'.

If your big idea is something that lots of people are going to want – the lightbulb, say, or the horseless carriage – then you might be up for some serious cash. But if your idea is something like 'I think therefore I am', the financial angle is limited.

Philosophers need to sell books and give lectures in order to make money. This is where dumbing it down might help. You need a catchphrase or a theory. Something like 'existence precedes essence' or 'beyond good and evil'.

Musicians, artists, and writers can make a good living. And these days, technology can help you. Beethoven and Mozart gave concerts or got commissions to earn their crusts. They didn't have the advantage of CDs, DVDs or downloads that they could sell like Britney Spears. Try to like your children, because when you're dead the royalties are theirs.

One final tip: if you're looking to make money as a physicist or a chemist, then nuclear and biological weapons are currently a good earner. You just need the right connections in order to be able to flog the stuff.

CHAPTER FIVE

Maximise Your Potential

'Genius lies not in thinking of ideas, but in the ability to execute the ideas.'

JANE MCELYEA

MAXIMISE YOUR POTENTIAL

YOU MIGHT BE THINKING THAT EITHER YOU'RE A GENIUS OR YOU'RE NOT. NICE AND SIMPLE. BUT YOU COULDN'T BE FURTHER FROM THE TRUTH. THERE ARE A NUMBER OF STEPS YOU CAN TAKE TO INCREASE THE LIKELIHOOD OF BLOSSOMING INTO A FIRST-CLASS INTELLECTUAL. BE SURE TO STRIDE THOSE STEPS.

The right kind of surname

As with many aspects of the world of genius, chance has a hand to play even in the story of the actual name that lives forever. Regardless of your brilliant achievement/discovery/invention, a name has to be pretty robust to last forever.

It's probably no accident that the spirit of genius prefers to brush its stardusty fingers against the brows of people with names that stand out. Genius wants memorable. Smith or Jones? Sound like geniuses? Mozart or Michelangelo? You've got to be rare.

TOP FIVE MAGICAL MODIFIERS

- **The Impaler.** This has simplicity, directness and threat. But you do sound a little like a one-trick pony.

- **The Terrible.** Bluntly put, this one doesn't do it anymore. We live with worldwide terror now. We're too used to it.

- **The Magnificent.** Still good to go, this majestical moniker is general enough to let people's imaginations do the work.

- **The Elder.** It's low-key and classy, it acknowledges your experience and wisdom, but it's probably too understated for the brash 21st century.

- **The Mongoose.** You could go left field and quirky. Though you could also end up sounding like a cartoon character.

Genius jobs

There is a decent range of jobs available to the aspirant intellectual mega-being: from third-rate teacher in a technical college to friend of the most powerful rulers. The tip here is that the top brass, like most of us, are keen on showbiz. So, being the pre-eminent playwright of the Renaissance is going to get you into more of those glossy majesty-and-gleaming-pomp parties than coming up with some linguistic theory about universal grammar.

Year zero

A number of geniuses have started their professional careers in dead-end jobs, only to be rocketed suddenly to the august surroundings of the Royal Society or an echoing papal antechamber. The message here is that if you are currently an unrecognised genius and you're getting a bit worried about how long you've been working as a post-office sorter or bank clerk, stay calm. Fate's finger may yet point you out.

On the other hand, an early start is always good. If you can get a job at an early age working for the king or the emperor or whoever the transient power figure is, all the better. Someone has to pay for all those operas and tragedies; someone has to cover your rent and your groceries while you're thinking the thoughts you need to think. Friends with deep pockets. And it's not really being a parasite – humanity needs you to get on.

A cautionary word about teamwork

Combining genius and teamwork is a dangerous operation. The public wants a single soul to glorify. So we're all supposed to understand that both Crick and Watson figured out the double helix DNA thing? 'Well, which one of them figured it out?' asks the head-scratching public, trying to visualise the two of them hunched over a lab bench, test tubes in the background, chatting about complicated stuff, and both realising something at exactly the same time. The teamwork reputation is never safe. Someone probably did take minutes after all. It's your word against theirs. Much safer to be the lone genius.

Unmanned genius

Darkest history does allow a kind of forgiveness and compromise. Lots of early literature is a collective enterprise, rounded and polished over generations before anyone thought of writing it down. And some of it manages to stand the test of time as great work. Homer's *Iliad* may not all be Homer's *Iliad*, but Homer's *Iliad* it is. *Gilgamesh*? *Beowulf*? Great titles, cultural stepping-stones and all, but who gets the credit? Someone missed an opportunity. The populace will always be uncomfortable with it. It's not the solitary act of heroic greatness that they want. They want a name.

Enter the left-field amateur

A risky but satisfying strategy is to appear suddenly from nowhere. There is a certain aspect of this in genius itself because of its ability to break new ground where no one had previously managed it. The point is that you don't have to be sponsored by an emperor or the church or anything. You can be the genius equivalent of the sleeper cell: making preparations, sharpening your idea and waiting for your moment.

It is important to stay focused during this period of intellectual exile. Be sure that your colleagues at the institute are all going to comment on how you were 'destined for greatness' and 'just different from everyone else'. Making that sudden lurch for greatness can be a strain, so be certain that you and those around you are ready. But don't make an idiot of yourself. What you have is not the X-factor; it's something else entirely.

Be optimistic

Consider the poet William Blake. He received hardly any recognition during his lifetime. He wasn't taught painting through apprenticeship like your average arty genius; in fact, he was taught by a man who came to him in his dreams. His poetry was seen as crazily idiosyncratic and marginal. It is. And we like that today, even if in 1800 it was seen as nonsense. He deserves credit, though. He remained convinced throughout his life that one day the world would get it. He was right.

ALBERT EINSTEIN (1879–1955) – PHYSICIST

- It took baby Einstein about four years to start talking, and young Einstein could be a difficult and rebellious child.

- Although Einstein was born in Ulm, Germany, he became a Swiss citizen in 1901 and an American citizen in 1940.

- Einstein first published his famous theory of relativity (including the mass–energy equivalence $E=mc^2$) in 1905; however, he had written the ideas in an essay ten years earlier, at the age of 16.

- Einstein's idea that gravitational field should influence the wavelength of light emitted by atoms was proven by observations of a 1919 eclipse.

- In 1939 Einstein signed a letter to President Franklin Roosevelt, written by physicist Leó Szilárd, suggesting that the U.S. government should develop the atom bomb before Germany did. After World War II, however, he lobbied for nuclear disarmament.

- In 1952 he was offered the presidency of Israel. He declined.

Dress the part

'Beauty like hers is genius' – Dante Gabriel Rossetti

There is no single dress code for geniuses. You have to make a judgment about what is appropriate in what context. This, however, is not as simple as it sounds. Even though it is still quite simple.

That tie with *those* shorts?

A toga or a codpiece might be fine in certain circumstances (though you might feel more comfortable collecting your Nobel Prize in the creased and shiny old suit that you bought for your first day of work). It's not always easy for a genius to know what is appropriate, but keeping things straightforward is the key. The lab coat is good for working in the lab, looking down the microscope, doing a double take then looking again, and all that. For expounding your theory to skeptical peers in the university library, a worn-out corduroy sports jacket over unironed shirt, with checked tie and navy V-neck will usually work. Remember to wear trousers and shoes also. For leading the hordes across the steppes in a sweep of mass murder, arson, and pillage, plenty of animal-hide combinations and a few trinkets made from the skulls and teeth of your vanquished foes. All these suggestions are simple but appropriate.

Act the part

Whether you're an attic-dwelling artistic genius, or a dungeon-dwelling mathematical genius, you will need to act the part. People expect it. And besides, it's being yourself.

If you are the artistic-genius-type, your role is to investigate the human condition. This may involve debauched and 'alternative' sexual behaviours, huge gambling debts, syphilis, mental health problems, and an early grave. It appeals to a romantic notion we have about creativity and social skills.

Do not disturb

At the other end of the spectrum you may need to be aloof, above the merely human. Your genius thinking might be about maths or physics, in which case your behaviour should eschew human relationships and their messy illogicality. Smudgy human relationships are a distraction from the stratospheric realm of pure numerical relationships.

If you must have human contact and friendship, find someone with whom you can talk equations. You should be able to locate at least one other person who cares what x is. Better to spend most of your time in front of a blackboard, chalk in hand, stacking up those big numbers and letters that stand for numbers in ever-more-complex combinations. A good sum is like a neat refrain from a Bach cantata – detailed, beautiful and rigorous. It's your instrument – play that thing!

REHEARSE SOME LINES

Here are a few things that might be uttered by a genius. Try them on for size.

- 'You're overlooking one small but essential fact, professor.'
- 'Parmenion will advance the troops at my command!'
- 'Cappuccino to go, please, Raoul.'
- 'I'm like, "Put the poker down, dude".'
- 'Thomas, when you advance, draw your sword straightaway. Think motivation. You're going to murder the king, darling.'
- 'And the process gives off a gas. A vapour of startling odour, which, when inhaled, brings forth feelings of extraordinary peculiarity. Try it.'
- 'This creature could destroy me. My work!'

Or . . .

- 'Eureka!'
- 'I think therefore I am.'
- 'You're a monkey.'
- 'Mistakes are the portals of discovery.'
- 'I refute it thus!'
- 'Thank you, madam, the agony is abated.'
- 'It is not enough to succeed. Others must fail.'

You will have noticed that some of the rehearsal statements end with punctuation signalling exclamation. Don't doubt it – part of the attraction of being a genius is the excitement. Just ask Archimedes. He got so excited by his groundbreaking idea that he ran naked through the streets.

CHAPTER SIX

Genius at Large

———◆———

'Genius . . . means the transcendent capacity
of taking trouble.'

THOMAS CARLYLE

GENIUS AT LARGE

BELIEVE IT OR NOT, PEOPLE SOMETIMES DON'T WANT TO HEAR WHAT A GENIUS HAS TO SAY. YOU SHOULD BEAR THIS IN MIND IF YOUR PARTICULAR GENIUS INVOLVES DELIVERING, ON BEHALF OF ALL OF HUMANITY, SOME UNCOMFORTABLE TRUTHS.

Muzzled

Sometimes it's not that they won't listen; it's that they are not allowed to listen. Take Galileo, for instance. He dared to publish a comparison of the Ptolemaic and Copernican systems and concluded, convincingly, that Copernicus was right – everything revolves around the sun. This was not a view popular with the church, and Galileo's judgment that he would probably get away with it turned out to be of the non-genius order. He was under house arrest for the rest of his days.

You can prove it

One reason the church was so uncomfortable with Galileo was that he stepped into a conceptual no-go zone. Galileo, a highly respected and accomplished man, crossed the line and said, 'No. It is not theory; it is *true*. The earth is not the centre of the universe. The maths proves it'. That's what the church didn't like. The 'it's true' bit and the 'maths proves it' bit.

Badge of honor

From the middle of the 16th century, the Catholic church published a list of works that printers were not allowed to produce. Perhaps slightly embarrassing for Popes Paul IV, Pius IV, Leo XIII, and so on, is that a good number of the books on the *Index Librorum Prohibitorum* are now seen as landmarks in the history of intellectual development.

The Index

Yes, the *Index Librorum Prohibitorum*. The books the Vatican thought you shouldn't read. It's a veritable Who's Who of brain power, the cream of the crop. Banned and proud.

1. **Nicolaus Copernicus.** Why would he be banned? He dedicated *De Revolutionibus Orbium Coelestium* to the Pope. Did they think he was being ironic?

2. **René Descartes.** *Thinking about God* is a tricky one. In one way the church does want you to think about God. But to think about God in other ways is not to be encouraged.

3. **Desiderius Erasmus.** Poor old Erasmus, surely not banned for the seemingly harmless title *The Praise of Folly*.

4. **Galileo Galilei.** The earth goes round the sun? Ban him!

5. **Immanual Kant.** Banned for the *Critique of Pure Reason*. Enough with the critiquing of pure reason, already.

6. **Niccolò Machiavelli.** His name is enough to give you the creeps.

7. **John Stuart Mill.** What Mill is doing is taking ideas about liberty and morality away from the church. He is on their turf and they are not going to stand for it.

Some people just don't like a brainiac

A current problem in our schools is the idea that learning is not 'cool'. This is, in a sense, a big idea. Its effect is certainly big. But it is not a genius idea. It is a foolish idea. It is evidence of a point of view that has dogged the advancement of mankind and the development of individual genius.

Many societies have (probably) shown a broad streak of anti-intellectualism whereby the intellectual is feared because of his or her superior knowledge. He or she might be able to prove that your understanding of the forces that shape your existence is limited. No one likes that. And sometimes, if people don't like you, they do something about it.

Some people simply hate a brainiac

Hypatia of Alexandria, charismatic teacher of mathematics and philosophy, was probably murdered by Christians who felt threatened by her Neoplatonist views. Socrates also managed to annoy too many people with his cheeky questioning and his philosophising. Death by hemlock for him.

The ability to die by being murdered is particularly noteworthy in the case of the political or leadership genius. Especially if, like the probably poisoned Ivan the Terrible, you have made enemies aplenty through a personal policy of orgiastic excess and a public policy of mass murder. But then he's not such a good example. He wasn't a genius. He was a nut.

HYPATIA OF ALEXANDRIA (370–415 C.E.) – PHILOSOPHER

- Employed in the Temple of the Muses at the Great Library of Alexandria, Hypatia's father was Theon, an astronomer, mathematician and teacher. He taught his daughter.

- Victorians Charles Kingsley and Charles William Mitchell were fascinated by Hypatia. Kingsley wrote a novel based on her life and she was the inspiration for Mitchell's most notable painting.

- She lectured on Platonist philosophy in Alexandria and Athens and attracted students from all over the Greek world.

- In her role as a teacher, Hypatia once had to deter a student who had fallen in love with her by throwing sanitary towels repeatedly at him.

- There exist different theories about her death, but Hypatia seems to have been murdered by a mob that was determined to silence such an influential pagan in what was becoming an increasingly Christian culture.

- One historian, Bishop John of Nikiu, perhaps wanting to ingratiate himself with Cyril, Bishop of Alexandria at the time of Hypatia's death, portrays her as a witch, beguiling men and leading them away from the church.

The late-in-life genius

The idea that you can discover your hidden genius in your twilight years is a bit of a myth. It is possible that after a lifetime of dedicated work as a moderately successful civil servant you might retire and think about writing the novel that you always felt was in you but you just never had time for, what with the job, the family, and the mortgage. You might write that novel and craft it over the next five years, so that when you send it to a publisher and you become a worldwide publishing sensation, you are already in your 70s. You are then lauded by the literary elite as that rare thing – the as-yet-undiscovered genius. So to die of a heart attack at the age of 68, only days before an interview for a big feature in the *New York Times*, seems a bit sad. It is sad. Avoid it.

The outsider

- Tormented by mental illness
- Ground down by poverty, lack of success, and stubbornness
- Driven to cut off part of his own ear and give it to a prostitute
- Thirty-seven years old when he shot himself in the chest in a field

It can only be Vincent van Gogh. On the very verge of going big, the manic redhead decided he couldn't take it. Sometimes the genius life is sad and short.

Getting recognised and avoiding execution at all costs

If, by this time, you've realised you are a source of dazzling, world-shaking ideas, you will need to get those ideas disseminated. Your primary aim at this point is to get publicity. Once your genius is recognised, you will have a serious profile. You may well make enemies. Here are ten tips for achieving your primary aim at this point – staying alive:

- Get to know an emperor or a pope or a Florentine prince. You need sponsorship to get your stuff out there.

- Persevere.

- Don't cross the Athenian people or the Christian church.

- Have some sophistry ready, in case the authorities come for you.

- Persevere.

- If you absolutely must court controversy, make sure to keep it inside the department.

- Get your dad involved.

- Be sure that you're not just nuts rather than a proper genius.

- In general, keep your eccentricities unthreatening.

- Persevere.

CHAPTER SEVEN

The Evil Genius

'The belief in a supernatural source of evil is
not necessary; men alone are quite capable
of every wickedness.'

JOSEPH CONRAD

THE EVIL GENIUS

EVIL IS REALLY NOT SOMETHING THAT SHOULD BE ENCOURAGED. IF YOU ARE AN INTELLECTUAL SUPER-BEING YOU SHOULD BE THINKING ABOUT HOW TO PUT YOUR BRILLIANCE TO USE FOR THE GOOD OF HUMANITY. BUT IF YOU'RE NASTY AND YOU KNOW IT, READ ON.

A question of morality

Ambition doesn't require a basis in morality – just ask Macbeth. Machiavelli will tell you that having morals can positively be a hindrance. Certainly, in terms of leadership, a lack of moral scruples can be a real bonus.

Foster your ruthlessness streak

Leadership is where evil genius really comes into its own. That's because leadership is about manipulating people, not numbers, shapes, or chemicals. People are affected by morality in ways that numbers, shapes and chemicals are not. An equilateral triangle has no moral resonance (unless it's a love triangle, but even then it's a metaphor). Similarly, it's hard to see a trapezoid as evil or Mendeleyev's table of elements as morally bankrupt and wicked.

If you are all about power, people will be prepared to fight you for that power, and you will have to be prepared to fight back. But then again, the cut and thrust isn't limited solely to the worlds of political and military might. You might have enemies in the chemistry department. There might be people who want to see your professional career fail. A touch of ruthlessness of character never went amiss for even the best of the good-hearted geniuses.

NICCOLÒ MACHIAVELLI (1469–1527) – POLITICAL PHILOSOPHER, MUSICIAN, POET, PLAYWRIGHT

- Only very few geniuses get to have their names turned into an adjective – 'Machiavellian' means cunning, opportunistic, and deceitful. For a Machiavellian character, the ends justify the means.

- *Il Principe* (*The Prince*) is Machiavelli's most famous work. It is an analysis of the manipulation of political power and marks a shift from the idealism of Plato to a new Renaissance realism.

- As a Florentine diplomat for over a decade, Machiavelli was well placed to study the turbulent political atmosphere of his day and to meet its major figures. He was particularly inspired by Cesare Borgia.

- In his text *Discorsi* (*Discourses*), Machiavelli sets out a series of lessons on how a republic should be established, structured, and governed. His brilliant political philosophy underpins many democracies today.

- In 1513 he was tortured on the rack for his alleged role in a political plot, but maintained his innocence. He was pardoned but exiled, where he continued writing his treatises.

- As a true Renaissance man, Machiavelli also wrote plays. His racy satirical comedy *La Mandragola* (*The Mandrake*) was a hit.

The monster's tale

Genius – particularly scientific genius – is haunted by the specter of 'Frankenstein's monster'. Frankenstein's monster represents the unforeseen effect, the arrogant genius losing possession of his or her ever-more-uncontrollable creation.

For example, the ability to split the atom soon led to military ramifications. Marie Curie was, in a tragedy of the Aristotelian sense, laid low by her own achievement – though not through hubris. Despite being the first woman to receive a Nobel Prize, her death was most probably caused by exposure to the radioactive materials she discovered. The irony is that Curie was caught in the Frankenstein narrative even though she was not an evil genius. So be warned that your good genius work could morph into evil genius material. You might start off wondering if an atom can be split and end up showing a general what happens when you do.

Frankenstein's Monster Syndrome

- Avoid selling your soul in exchange for instant fame
- Don't buy a medieval castle in the Carpathians
- Stop the experiment if you start to feel guilt mixing with the arrogance
- Ask yourself if it really is for the good of mankind
- Try not to focus solely on 'the power to create life itself!'

Can tyrants be geniuses?

'My presence scares happiness away; and good deeds grow powerless, when I become concerned in them. Fugitive, unresting I should be, that my evil genius might not seize me . . . ' – J. W. Goethe

The question is whether wickedly evil tyrants can display genius characteristics. And the answer has to be yes, though they're few and far between. The thing about the evil tyrant-style genius, if you're considering such a career path, is that it's really difficult to make your mark in an immortal, genius kind of way. There are, observably, different levels of tyranny, and you stand out by being the most murderous or the cruellest killer. But is this genius? Someone like Robert Mugabe is a fairly successful tyrant, but quite obviously not a genius. The question, or one question, is whether the exercise of an outstanding intellect can be seen in the actions of a wicked despot.

Was Stalin a genius? Was Hitler a genius? Our judgment here is all about power management and strategic acumen. Were Hitler and Stalin demonstrating outstanding intellect when they turned their enemies against each other and consolidated their control? No. They were just clever bullies writ large. It probably wasn't an act of genius to purge the Soviet army's officers on the eve of German invasion. It probably wasn't an act of genius to delay the southerly movement of the panzers because the Normandy landings appeared to be a feint. (Although we should keep in mind that having stupid ideas doesn't necessarily disqualify you from genius status. Newton, of all people, was convinced that alchemy was a viable pursuit.) The big two despots of the 20th century were ruthless, evil and had bucketloads of cunning. But that didn't make them geniuses.

Isn't it good to be feared?

Admiration and awe are what you're really going for when you sign up for genius status. They are often enjoyable consequences of genius and occasionally form strong workable motivational tools as you work late into the night on your genius concepts.

But fear is a different thing. Fear as an end in itself or as a means of controlling people's lives somehow doesn't quite sit with being a genius. Fear is the means by which tyrants stop their subjects thinking or talking about new ideas. But geniuses like new ideas. If a tyrant does like a new idea it is probably a new idea about how to kill enemies, destroy their citadels, and lay waste their lands. This is all right, but can be a bit of a bore. From the bow and arrow to the laser-guided bomb, it's all about killing people. So don't throw your life's work into ways of exterminating others if only because it's been done so much before. It's not exactly akin to a revelation like 'species adapt to their environments through a process of evolution' or 'for a right-angle triangle with legs a and b and hypotenuse c, $a^2+b^2 = c^2$'. Is it?

One of us

The ideal combination, if despotism and tyranny are your thing, is to be admired by your people and feared by your enemies. Where your enemies regard you as aggressive and brutal, your people must see you as strong and confident. Following are some thinking points for the aspiring evil genius.

Retain your reason

Despite the fact that you are insanely evil, you still need reason. Consider Stalin's use of equation: death solves all problems; therefore, no man = no problem. Very simple, very 'big picture', very cause and effect. Totally evil too, of course.

Become a cult figure

Once you achieve power you should get yourself mythologised. This often happens to geniuses once they are dead, but you need to get it happening sooner. Achieve this by setting up a ministry of propaganda, inventing proverbial episodes from your childhood, and ensuring that every sculpture is of you.

Your attitude towards violence

You will either need to feel ambivalent towards violence or to actually like it. When Napoleon said that the carnage at

Borodino was 'the most beautiful battlefield I've ever seen', he meant it.

You're the team captain

As a ruthless leader, you will need the help of others – flunkies, sycophants, yes-men. You will at times have to delegate power. Your genius is for managing those who exercise power on your behalf, creating structures of political machinery that allow you control. Go, Captain!

You're history

'The man of genius . . . is an originator, an inspired or
demonic man, who produces a perfect work in obedience
to laws yet unexplored.' – Henry David Thoreau

The evil genius is probably not remembered for a series of
world-changing ideas. It's no accident that Plato's philosopher
kings are ideal rather than real rulers. The evil genius is
remembered as one of history's do-ers rather than as one of
science or philosophy's thinkers.

You might be remembered by some colourful sobriquet.
Who wouldn't want to be remembered as, say, Jeremy 'the
Impaler' or Peaches 'the Merciless'? But these adjectival
accessories really only serve to point out that you were
Terrible or Great, not that you thought anything new. King
Richard gets remembered for his Lionheart rather than his
Godbrain. Even the mysterious 'Genghis Khan' only means
Genghis the Chief.

CHAPTER EIGHT

Genius and Romance

'Beware you are not swallowed up in books!
An ounce of love is worth a pound
of knowledge.'

JOHN WESLEY

GENIUS AND ROMANCE

OBVIOUSLY, THE QUESTION ON EVERYONE'S LIPS IS HOW BEING A GENIUS AFFECTS YOUR LOVE LIFE. IS BEING A BRAINIAC GOING TO GET YOU THE GIRL OR GUY? OF COURSE, EROS, *AMOUR* — WHATEVER YOU WANT TO CALL IT — WILL ALSO ENSURE THAT THERE ARE TIMES WHEN THE HEART RULES THE HEAD. YOU MIGHT THINK THAT'S BAD FOR SOMEONE WHO IS ALL ABOUT BRAIN POWER. YOU MIGHT BE RIGHT.

The IQ aphrodisiac

Dinner with a mad-professor type? What comes to mind? An absence of romantic mood, lashings of social ineptitude, a funny voice prattling on about quasars and dark matter?

Consider the Jerry Lewis film *The Nutty Professor*. The alchemic 'potion' the professor drinks turns him from the geekishly nerdy Professor Julius Kelp into the slick and sensual Buddy Love. The lothario and the intellectual are presented as opposites. But the film's message, thankfully for us all, is that it doesn't have to be that way. Intellectuals are attractive for what they are. Knowledge is power. Power is attractive.

The few successful ones

Blanket assertions aside (or in theoretical parentheses), there may be problems balancing intellectual activity and *la vie d'amour*. It really does depend on your chosen field.

Shakespeare got to hang out with aristocrats and the theater crowd. (It should be remembered that there were no actresses in 1600, so theatre was yet to become the hotbed of dressing-room shenanigans that it is today). Dickens liked to get out and meet his adoring fans through public readings. His mistress was an actress. Picasso set the standard though – a ballerina, an artist, a photographer – all sorts of complicated offspring stuff. So focusing on the performing or visual arts seems a good bet if your intellectual curiosity has a smoochy side.

Love in the lab

The lab is a place of work and as such as good a place as any to meet a spouse. But be realistic. The prospective bedmate you meet in a lab is unlikely to be a countess or a love-crazed bohemian. More likely an assistant or a cleaner.

As a literary genius, you might pen a number of love sonnets, which will be gold dust in any long-distance epistolary seduction. As an artistic genius, you may paint a portrait of the object of your desire that leaves no doubt as to the depth and authenticity of your love. However, collecting your own urine, letting it putrefy, and then heating it to condense its vapours all in the name of scientific investigation is less adaptable in terms of using the product of your intellect to attract mates.

The problem of remembering your spouse's name

If you were Picasso, you could be forgiven for forgetting your spouse's name. For heaven's sake, he married so many. However, for most geniuses the problem is more to do with having your mind over-crammed with difficult stuff. It's easy for something as mundane as the name of your spouse or firstborn to disappear under a mountain of far-more-important detail. It is therefore advisable for prospective geniuses to carry an index card listing useful names and addresses – including their own.

WILLIAM SHAKESPEARE (1564–1616)
– PLAYWRIGHT, POET, ACTOR

- Born the son of a glover and civic official, William had two brothers and four sisters.

- At the age of 19, he married Anne Hathaway, who was 26 years old and pregnant.

- Legend has it that he ran away to London because he was caught poaching. But Shakespeare was not a bad businessman and it might be more likely that he went to London to make money.

- As well as writing about 38 plays and more than 150 sonnets and other poems, Shakespeare acted too and is known to have performed for Queen Elizabeth I.

- Speculation continues as to whether William Shakespeare from Stratford did indeed write all of the works attributed to him. Candidates for alternative authorship include the playwright Christopher Marlowe; Edward de Vere, Earl of Oxford; and philosopher and statesman Sir Francis Bacon.

- Just as Shakespeare was building a reputation as a playwright, London theatres were closed down because of the plague in 1593. Shakespeare stayed in the capital but switched to poetry for a while.

The Mrs. Einstein syndrome

Just as in domestic life, it might be that, professionally your partner is your competitor. This could be a problem. Why? Well, do you want to share your Nobel Prize?

Consider the case of the man who came to exemplify genius in the 20th century. A series of groundbreaking and physics-reshaping publications established Einstein as the big boss of understanding the universe. Or did it? Might he have been assisted by someone whom history did not choose to deify? Might that person have been his first wife, Mileva Marić? Possibly, but probably not. She was a brainy, scientific type and she may have helped Albert out, but the evidence that they collaborated in-depth is scant.

And since you're wondering, the case for an Einstein conspiracy is flimsy. It is known that he discussed ideas with two other physics fans, Conrad Habicht and Maurice Solovine (quite good genius names, but not top-notch). The three men formed a little discussion group they called the Olympia Academy. But it seems they discussed . . . philosophy.

What the comfy slippers of cultural remembering wants is the story of the puppet and the puppet mistress. A conspiracy version. But unfortunately this isn't the case. The moral of the story goes something like: 'marry a moron'. That way, the historians and hagiographers can be sure it was all your own work and there will be no tarnish on your shiny reputation.

Unlucky in love

In case this genius caper isn't working out for you, there's some consolation to be felt in the fact that many geniuses are notoriously unlucky in love. Nineteenth-century philosophy buff Friedrich Nietzsche might have been a brilliant thinker but he was on the Loserville Express when it came to the ladies.

Nietzsche may have suffered repeated rejection because he was a gloomy and manic kind of guy. He was also probably done in by syphilis, possibly contracted from a prostitute that he claims he was forced to sleep with when university pals kidnapped him and took him to the best little whorehouse in Saxony. Those crazy intellectuals!

The genius of love

However, it's just possible that you might be thinking that love itself is your field of expertise. This is what Giovanni Giacomo Casanova thought. In his time he worked for the church and the army and was a diplomat, spy, writer, businessman and amateur philosopher. But passion was his real passion, and he's remembered as being the genius of love in a way that rock 'n' rollers, actors, and other artistes are not. This is because, for him, seduction and sex were not perks of the trade, they *were* the trade. In his autobiography he claims to have slept with more than 120 women. He has the right kind of name to be a genius, but what was his big idea? 'Sleeping with lots of people is good'? Hardly seems original.

Seduction tips

Should you desire to seduce another genius, consider the following approaches:

- When you meet a fellow mega-mind say things like, 'Your ideas make me . . . hot' or 'IQ scores are so erotic'.

- Wear low-cut lab coats.

- Hang out in galleries, fainting occasionally.

- Hang out at the Patent Office, fainting occasionally.

- Hang out at the CERN Accelerator Complex, fainting for an incomprehensibly brief period of time.

Love and the punishing schedule

While aspiring to Casanova heights of romance, remember that sometimes a punishing love schedule can interfere with the punishing schedule of being a genius.

In the case of the Marquis de Sade, philosopher and pornographer (a rare but impressive combination), the big idea was that nature shows no morality and thus morality is unnatural. (If he was so keen on being 'natural', one wonders why he bothered living in a house or wearing clothes). He thus pursued a life of amoral sexual pleasure, which gained him an enviable notoriety. But while Nietzsche – a dismal failure in the game of love – is remembered for his brain stuff, de Sade – bedding bevies of babes daily – is not remembered for the lifechanging ideas he bequeathed to us, but just for really walking the walk. His most famous book has two titles: *One Hundred Days of Sodom* or *The School of Freedoms*. By which do you think it is remembered?

The point is that if you are a thinker and a mad sexual libertine at the same time, the public, being the ravenous scandal puppies they are, may overlook your ideas. This is not what you want. If you are an amoral sex machine, keep it out of the papers.

How to be both a lover and a thinker

The next time you are at an intimate soirée, you might like to try out some of the following lines. Not all of them will be appropriate. Context will help you judge.

- 'Yes, my dear, but I was thinking of a different kind of chemistry.'

- 'I can paint you as you'd like to see yourself.'

- 'My mind may be with the wind-blown clouds, but other parts of me are closer to earth.'

- 'Come to my garret and I'll show you the stars.'

- 'If you'll meet me at my lab, I need someone to hold my Bunsen burner.'

- 'You are the aria in my opera, the sonata in my symphony. Let me call you "No. 45".'

- 'I'm working on an alternative political philosophy for establishing a republic in this time of social upheaval and global turmoil. But I sometimes take breaks. Got time for a cappuccino?'

- 'I speak 18 languages. I can't say "no" in any of them.'

- 'I'll take over a country for you, my love. Take your pick.'

- 'Eureka, baby!'

CHAPTER NINE

On Being
Remembered

—◆—

'Here lies one whose name was
written in water.'

JOHN KEATS'S EPITAPH

ON BEING REMEMBERED

THERE'S LITTLE POINT IN BEING A GENIUS IF YOU DON'T GET YOUR PAGE IN THE GREAT BOOK OF HUMAN PROGRESS. DON'T BE LIKE KEATS. GET YOURSELF SOME REPUTATION.

Overnight enlightenment

It is long past midnight. The night is cold and the wind whips the attic roof and rattles the loose skylight. On the little writing table, the candle gutters, its yellow light dancing on the green glass of an empty wine bottle. You are hunched over your parchment, coughing and wheezing and sniffing and trying to finish a sonnet about the physical manifestation of passion in first love. At the back of your mind quotidian worries push against your poetic imagination. You have no money for food or rent and don't know where you will get it. You have coughed up blood again today. Another of the many voices in your head indignantly repeats what it always says: 'This isn't right. You are a genius'.

And then . . .

The following week, the earl of Daventry is sending a carriage to collect you from your hotel. You have spent the afternoon in your suite being soft-soaped, shaved, and rubbed down by a most comely young woman provided by the maitre d'hotel, and the earl's physician has made a brief visit, during which he counseled you to put worry aside – for the prognosis is good – and has made an appointment for some blood-letting next week. The earl's carriage takes you to the townhouse salon of Countess Daphne of Huntingdon, where you are to give a private reading from your new and extensive collection of mock-classical lyrics.

Once at the salon, and having read your work to warm appreciation and applause, you are introduced to a number of most attractive actresses, poets from Paris, painters from Prague, and playwrights from Philadelphia. Each declares you to be in possession of a rare kind of genius. You have a series of fascinating conversations, drinking the countess's delightful sherry and smoking some fine tobacco newly shipped from Virginia. It is a thoroughly pleasurable evening.

The denouement

But now the smoke is too much and breathing becomes difficult. Why is everyone laughing and drinking and smiling when you can hardly breathe? The reason is that you are not at the townhouse salon. You are still in your garret and you have lapsed into unconsciousness. You cannot breathe because the candle has set fire to the sheaf of poems on the table and now the table itself, and the filthy, ragged curtains are burning fiercely, filling your domicile with dense fumes. You half-manage to wake yourself. The smoke and flames are now so thick and fierce that it is difficult to find your bearings. It occurs to you that you may die. Yes, being catapulted to fame is only a dream.

Wake up to the dream

'Never expect any recognition here – the system prohibits it. The cross is not affixed to the genius, no, the genius is affixed to the cross.' – Franz Grillparzer

It's a dream that has 21st-century western culture in its thrall. And it's easy to buy into. You just need to be on television in order for people to think you're some kind of genius. But being on television probably means you're not a genius. While genius often means fame, fame rarely means genius. Cultural achievement, even if you're Mozart, takes a while and some practice to get going. If you're not out and about getting your reputation going, you run the risk of posthumous recognition without a scrap of contemporary adoration, or 'doing a Franz Kafka', as it's known.

This problem, however, is less evident in the sciences. If you happen to invent the pasteurisation process or publish a full table of elements then you get the job done in one go and you can sit back and sharpen your pencil. Like all sorts of stuff, it's about choice.

Slow-burning reputation and the waves of history

> 'If you are a genius and unsuccessful, everybody treats you as if you were a genius, but when you come to be successful . . . everybody no longer treats you like a genius, [but] like a man who has become successful.'
> – Pablo Picasso

Reputation, once bid farewell, is never seen again. So they say. But it's not true. Reputation can burn slowly for a time before it catches; it can be a rising and falling wave; it can be represented by any number of metaphors. You can almost disappear from the map of human knowledge, understanding, and creativity and still come charging back to greatness and glory. Your revelatory idea might fade, superseded by better, neater ideas, or it may become increasingly important as the decades and centuries roll by.

The test of time

Think of Charles Darwin and Karl Marx. Both massive names who earned their own adjectives. Their ideas infuse our thinking about ourselves, our societies, our relationships, our very humanity. You can't ask much more from a genius than that. But how have their reputations changed since those heady early days?

Darwin, with elegant understatement, uses the word 'evolve' only once in *Origin of Species*. It's the last word in the book. And threatening to be a last word, it's an idea that still draws people into heated arguments and acts of bizarre legislation today. The world's great religions know that it means them no good. Darwin knew it. We all know it.

Marx's ideas changed the lives of many more millions of people than Darwin in much more practical ways. And his ideas are still doing the rounds. You don't have to look too far into the third world to find a Marxist guerrilla movement or uprising. But Marx has lost ground. As a critical framework for historians, social scientists, and the like, Marxism is still a useful tool. As an ideological position in an actively political sense, it's got a dated feel.

So two genius hotshots have their big ideas interpreted in very different ways in very different eras. Beware the revisionist tendencies of those who come after you. Try to be cleverer than they are in order to be sure you come out on top.

Tomorrow and tomorrow . . .

Who knows what is to come? Who knows who we will be in centuries ahead? Perhaps ideas being thought at this very moment, this actual second – your ideas – will influence the lives of millions of future inhabitants of the earth. One thing we do know is that genius ideas never stop coming. Or they haven't so far.

Will the future leave you behind altogether and for good?

There's no doubt about it. Whether or not a genius is remembered, or indeed how that genius is remembered, changes according to contemporary fashion. This is most apparent in the arts, but can be apparent in the sciences too.

We are currently surrounded by 'genetic this' and 'genome that', so the DNA double-helix guys, Crick and Watson, still have serious reputation. And Darwin sits at the back of all this with an adoring chimp on his knee.

We also like physics, the mind-bending complexity of it and its promise to solve the big questions about the universe. Stephen Hawking is popular, not so much for what he says as for fitting in with our popular mythologies by being a futuristic half-machine-half-super-brain, the robotic voice of the atom age. Behind this sits Einstein, atop Newton's shoulders.

Avoid being a Faraday

We are a bit bored with other aspects of science, however. Just ask Michael Faraday. If you are fanatical about electricity then Faraday is your man. Very big in his day. Or Nikola Tesla, perhaps, whose ideas came to him in flashes of blinding light. Their problem is that you are probably not fanatical about electricity. Electricity has changed our lives, but does it change the way we think about our lives? The egghead of the

21st century doesn't want to make up electrical circuits in the back bedroom. That egghead is more likely to be writing some computer code and thinking that Bill Gates is a genius because he's the richest man in the universe and lives on his own moon.

Faraday's message to the young geniuses of today is that the future may take all your ideas and forget about you, or decide that your epiphanies are just not needed anymore.

Remembered, but not for the reasons you thought

Perhaps you expect to be remembered for your operas rather than your symphonies, or evermore lauded by literate lovers for your verse epics rather than your sonnets. It might not be so much of a surprise to you to find that the opposite occurs. Oh well, tastes change. You could probably get used to it.

But imagine yourself as a philosopher whose only desire is to be loved and published so you can get your ideas out there for other big brains to discuss over an espresso or two. Try hard. Keep imagining, so you can imagine how it would feel to look down from your cloud, only half a century after you shuffled off the coil, to see one of modern history's top crazy dictators using you and your name as supposed inspiration for more mad stuff. And you'd thought living with syphilis was bad enough.

MARIE SKLODOWSKA-CURIE (1867–1934) – PHYSICIST, CHEMIST

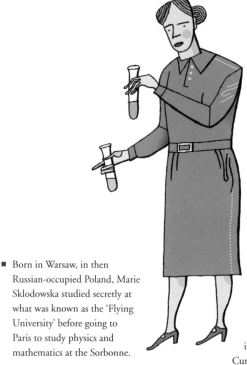

- Born in Warsaw, in then Russian-occupied Poland, Marie Sklodowska studied secretly at what was known as the 'Flying University' before going to Paris to study physics and mathematics at the Sorbonne.

- Marie married her tutor, Pierre Curie, and together they carried out pioneering work on radioactivity. They were the first to isolate the elements radium and polonium.

- The 1903 Nobel Prize for physics was awarded jointly to Marie, Pierre and Henri Becquerel for their work with radium. In 1911 Curie became the first person to be awarded Nobel Prizes in two fields, when she was awarded the prize for chemistry.

- After her husband was killed in a motor accident in Paris, Curie scandalised many by having an affair with one of her married colleagues.

- The element Curium is named after Marie and Pierre, as is the unit of radiation, the Curie.

- Her death was almost certainly brought about by long-term exposure to radiation. Her notes and papers are still radioactive and are stored in special containers.

CHAPTER TEN

The Legacy of Genius

———◆———

'No legacy is so rich as honesty.'

WILLIAM SHAKESPEARE

THE LEGACY OF GENIUS

VERY RICH FROM THE BARD, WHOSE ONLY LEGACY TO HIS WIFE WAS HIS SECOND-BEST BED! ANYWAY, NOW THAT YOU'RE SURE YOU'RE ON THE ROAD TO BEING A TOP-FLIGHT GENIUS, YOU NEED TO THINK ABOUT WHAT KIND OF HISTORICAL AND CULTURAL FOOTPRINT YOU'RE GOING TO LEAVE BEHIND. LET'S HOPE IT'S HUMAN.

Being a cultural icon

Have you got the look? Has your look ever been recorded? A variety of media will work – marble bust, oil on canvas, photograph, clay. You know what people are like: they like to be able to put a face to the name. If you're very lucky, your face can become iconic. Think Einstein, think Shakespeare, think Marx.

If your face is memorable, you're memorable. Think what you do with your facial hair to make yourself stand out or look intellectual. You might even be able to achieve icon status without using your own face. In an odd way, Michelangelo's statue *David* is Michelangelo. In an even odder way, the *Mona Lisa* is da Vinci.

Becoming iconic means that you end up representing more than just yourself or your ideas. You come to epitomise something about genius itself.

Cuddly Uncle Albert

Albert Einstein, today at least, epitomises the very centre of the kernel of the essence of genius. His ideas were radical, counterintuitive, and very complicated. Yet his image – most importantly the image of him as an old man – helps us not to feel intimidated by his greatness. He looks a bit unkempt, like a kindly grandparent, and he was famously photographed poking his tongue out, so he also has a nice, informal thing going on.

Modelling your look on Einstein's might seem like a sensible strategy, but it is difficult to pull off effectively – particularly if you are a woman. In addition, trying to look like Albert the Brainy will smack of imitation and lack of originality. These are not genius traits.

Will power

Shakespeare manages to epitomise a particularly important time in English history as well as English literature. An intellectual, cultural, and imperial explosion is beginning. Shakespeare puts it all in his plays. But his picture, in particular the Chandos portrait, also manages to represent the idea of the genius writer – observant, aloof, inscrutable.

The workers' beard

Marx is all about the beard. The beard itself, in a general sense rather than just Marx's, has long been a signifier of wisdom and experience. Marx uses it well. His full, impressive growth and gray halo make his head look big and thus full of knowledge and learning. The beard and the eyebrows shout their disregard for appearance ('appearance isn't truth, you fool!') and hint at long nights in the study leafing through many a weighty tome. The iconic image of Marx encapsulates the years of reading and thought a genius puts in – the head-cramming stuff.

'Oh, the razor guy!'

The other thing you can do is get yourself a memorable gimmick that is inseparable from your name. Occam's razor is memorable and arouses our curiosity. What did a mathematician want with a razor? Archimedes's principle is kind of memorable ('the buoyant force is equal to the weight of the displaced fluid' – catchy or what?) and Archimedes's screw sort of stays in the mind. But what we really all remember is Archimedes jumping out of his bath, the public nudity, and shouting, 'Eureka!' So get yourself a tagline, a catchphrase, or at the very least, a memorable accessory to attach to your big idea.

GENIUS GIMMICKS

Want to stand out from the genius crowd? Get yourself a gimmick.

- **Albert Einstein.** Einstein's gimmick was a rejection of the stuffy formality of academe. He chose to lecture in scruffy sweaters and carpet slippers.

- **Arthur Schopenhauer.** It is extreme, but Schopenhauer resorted to pushing old ladies down stairs. It's certainly quirky.

- **Diogenes.** Diogenes of Sinope deserves recognition for deciding that the way to distinguish himself from all those heavyweight Greek philosophers was to live in a barrel.

Why we need to believe in genius

If genius didn't exist we'd have to invent it. And perhaps we did. We certainly invented the word.

A bit of philology at this juncture might not do any harm. (Philology might seem like a big word, but it isn't really. It only has nine letters – the same as 'mushrooms'. Can't be that hard. Etymology if you prefer. Same number of letters. What is important is where the word came from.) 'Genius' is Latin (possibly related to *genie*, the Frenchified version of the Arabic *jinni* too) and it means 'guardian spirit of a person or place'.

So the term 'genius' already comes with a built-in godlike, superpower angle. But it only starts to mean what we want it to mean in the 17th century. The Enlightenment needed plenty of geniuses to cast off the gloomy intellectual cobwebs of the Dark Ages, so that's why this word turned up – to describe them.

Anything's possible

Suppose, however, that there is no such thing as genius. That there are only millions of people whose intellectual abilities run along a spectrum from astoundingly brilliant to unbelievably stupid. It starts to seem a little more like the lottery, only the odds are much worse.

Genius might not exist and might simply be an idea that we like and so believe in. There are two ideas here: someone will find the answer, and it might be me.

- Ludwig was the youngest of eight children born into a wealthy and cultured Viennese family. The Wittgensteins were often visited by artistic luminaries including Gustav Mahler and Johannes Brahms.

- A school photograph from the Realschule in Linz, Austria, shows teenage Wittgenstein sitting within a few feet of the teenage Adolf Hitler.

- Although a recognised philosophical genius, Wittgenstein published only one book, *Tractatus Logico-Philosophicus*. In it he outlined his groundbreaking philosophy of language and logic, which has significantly influenced the fields of psychology and psychotherapy.

- During World War I, Wittgenstein commanded an Austrian artillery battery. He was taken prisoner by the Italians, who allowed him to correspond with English philosophers from captivity. During World War II, he worked as a hospital porter in London.

- When his father died, Wittgenstein inherited the family fortune. He gave some of it away to Austrian artists and poets including Rainer Maria Rilke.

- Wittgenstein liked to live an ascetic lifestyle and, thinking that his *Tractatus* had solved all philosophical problems, became a primary school teacher and then a monastery gardener for a while. He was eventually lured back to teaching philosophy at Cambridge.

Ensuring the best encyclopedia entry

It's important to consider now how you want to be written up. Your historical footprint can be analysed according to its parts, its 'toes' studied individually. On each of these little piggies the chiropodist of biography will want to find the bunions of narrative. You need to consider origins, childhood, early career, romance, body of work, death.

Baby genius

Having unremarkable origins obviously doesn't mean you can't be a genius. Behind the gray net curtains of the suburban bungalow lurk many quiet boys and girls waiting for the fated opportunity that will carry them and their intellects away to more fertile ground. However, if you do have a boring background, the two most popular angles are the 'hot-housed by zealous parents' or the 'left to own devices' ones. Any television dramas made about you will appreciate this opportunity for a montage.

And then one day . . .

It's good to have an epiphanic childhood moment, when you realise what it is you want to do with that monumental talent of yours. Give it some setting. You might be up on a hill or at a cliff's edge or clinging to the spire of some gothic cathedral, somewhere high up, a nice godlike perch.

Crowds can work. The awesome scale of the blood-soaked battlefield makes a dramatic setting. But the childhood moment itself is basically all about lone discovery. If you must have other people present, keep it simple. The repeated rebukes of the memorable mentor or the dying words of the crazed beggar are often more resonant to the historian than the carnage of conquest over some now-abandoned city-state east of Persia – because they are simply simpler.

Extremity please

Extremity is best if you want to make it count with the biographers. They'll enjoy writing about your meetings with the emperor and your rapid rise through the court hierarchy or your soul-searching solitude in urban penury – leaky roofs, consumptive coughs, and all.

The matter of the heart

A turbulent romantic life is a great way to make a mark. Torrid affairs, bastard children, and domestic chaos give you the human factor. Everybody loves a rough diamond. The comforting narrative here is that brilliance and moral rectitude don't go hand in hand, so allowing Mr. and Mrs. Public to think either that in some way the great are no better than them, or that in some way they are disgustingly and intriguingly worse.

Be careful, though. Some 'romantic practices' might see you remembered not for your greatness but for your weirdness.

Your Nobel speech

The following is a cut-out-and-keep speech template for when you win your Nobel Prize. Simply cross out the options you don't want and you're ready to go.

'Ladies and gentlemen of the Academy, let me first thank you from the bottom of my heart for the great honour you bestow upon me. That I stand before you here today is all thanks to . . .

    a) God

    b) the collaboration and encouragement of colleagues

    c) the support of my lovely wife/partner and my family

    d) my own efforts

As a small . . .

    a) boy

    b) girl

I was always fascinated by . . .

    a) physics

    b) chemistry

    c) medicine

    d) literature

    e) peace

I would wander about my hometown, thinking about . . .

    a) how light travelled

    b) what air was made of

    c) why I had a headache

    d) whether words could describe what I could see

    e) how peaceful it was

They were formative days and filled me with a determination to . . .

    a) understand the universe

    b) get a chemistry set

    c) experiment with drugs

    d) learn to read

    e) live a quiet life

My life since then has been full of . . .

    a) misery

    b) joy

    c) opportunity

    d) difficulties

Achieving recognition for . . .

    a) discovering a theoretical particle

    b) creating a brand-new pollutant

    c) synthesising a new drug that cures acne/greed/embarrassment

    d) writing a novel about social injustice/globalisation/love in spite
       of a cultural divide/my own sex life

    e) bringing lasting peace to the Middle East

. . . is a dream come true. And having arrived at this exalted status, I
feel qualified to offer . . .

    a) some advice

    b) a warning

. . . to those aspiring to greatness in . . .

a) physics

b) chemistry

c) medicine

d) literature

e) peace

What you will undoubtedly need most is . . .

a) determination

b) luck

c) wealthy parents

d) a beard

In conclusion, I believe fundamentally that it is the role of the . . .

a) scientist

b) megalomaniac

c) writer

d) redundant politician

. . . to make the world a more . . .

a) physical

b) chemical

c) medicated

d) wordy

e) mellow

. . . place. Thank you.'

CHAPTER ELEVEN

Best in Show

'I am the greatest.'

MUHAMMAD ALI

BEST IN SHOW

SO WHO ARE THE BEST GENIUSES? AND WHO IS THE GENIUS'S GENIUS? IT'S TIME TO GET COMPARATIVE AND SUPERLATIVE. YOU CAN MEASURE GENIUS BY THE SIMPLE IQ TEST, OR YOU CAN LOOK AT THE PROFUNDITY OF WHATEVER IT IS YOUR GENIUS HAS DONE FOR THE CONSCIOUSNESSES OF HUMANITY. GENIUS IS A HUMAN QUALITY, SO YOU CAN'T EXPECT NICE, NEAT ANSWERS.

IQ, UQ, we all Q

The student of genius is presented with some particular problems when considering how the great ones are measured and categorised. Let's look at IQ.

Dr Catharine Morris Cox carried out some possibly unreliable research in 1926 to reveal how the fields of genius pan out in terms of IQ. So who are the big bosses of the G-word? Well, the lauded leaders of lofty intellect are not politicians, they're not scientists, they're not artists – they're philosophers. Yes, philosophers. By all sorts of questionable number crunching they come out with an average IQ of 160.

Oddly, the upper echelons of Cox's flight of researching fancy are not the household names you might expect. Who is the daddy of geniuses? Top dog is Johann Wolfgang von Goethe (210). You know, Goethe. Surely not that many days of your life pass between the conversational quoting of a couple of lines from Goethe's satanic closet drama, *Faust*?

Goethe was a writer and, on average, writers come down the list a bit. So what did Goethe do for humanity with his gargantuan IQ? Well, he was certainly a genius. Somewhat polymathic, Goethe was a little bit scientist, a little bit politician, but mostly poet and dramatist. (He was also nutty enough to attack Newton's ideas on optics and suggest that Napoléon Bonaparte was the saviour of European civilisation – the joke here is his thinking that European civilisation could be saved.) He even discovered the intermaxillary jawbone. In Germany he is rightly revered. But writers suffer from the great tribal difference that we call language. For the average non-German, it's easier to understand the genius of Rembrandt or Beethoven or even Einstein, because the problem of language doesn't intervene. Genius isn't always international.

Are you on the list?

The Morris Cox list has philosophers top, followed by scientists, writers, statesmen, musicians, artists and, last and least, soldiers. But the samples are different sizes, classical antiquity doesn't get a look in, and the whole thing is a sort of exercise in saying, 'Yes, geniuses are clever'. And the top flight tends to be polymaths, so the categories seem a bit blurred. That said, we all like a list. Goethe is followed by Emmanuel Swedenborg (scientist and philosopher), Gottfried Leibniz (rationalist philosopher, mathematician and politician), John Stuart Mill (liberal philosopher and political economist), and Blaise Pascal (mathematician, scientist and philosopher).

If you should feel disappointed by this top five, that's understandable. No artists, no musicians, no statesmen. It's a bit European, a bit Protestant, a bit male. Somehow the list doesn't satisfy. Thomas Chatterton and Sofia Kovalevskaya above Mozart and Copernicus? It's not a list to please the people.

IQ gives you a number. Goethe was 210, Einstein was a lowly 160! But what good is a number, really?

TOP 10 IQ CLUB

- **210** Johann Wolfgang von Goethe (1749–1832) German polymath (or know-it-all).

- **205** Emanuel Swedenborg (1688–1772) Swedish scientist, philosopher, mystic and theologian.

- **205** Gottfried Wilhelm von Leibniz (1646–1716) German polymath. Another know-it-all.

- **200** John Stuart Mill (1806–1873) British philosopher and political economist.

- **195** Blaise Pascal (1623–1662) French mathematician, physicist and religious philosopher.

- **190** Ludwig Wittgenstein (1889–1951) Austrian philosopher.

- **187** Bobby Fischer (1943–) U.S.-born Icelandic chess International Grandmaster and World Chess Champion.

- **185** Galileo Galilei (1564–1642) Italian physicist, astronomer, astrologer, philosopher. And heretic.

- **185** René Descartes (1596–1650) Founder of Modern Philosophy and Father of Modern Mathematics.

- **180** Madame de Staël (1766–1817) Swiss author. Also known as Anne Louise Germaine de Staël.

The unsolvable equation

So is any of this league table stuff any help? The arts and sciences all build on previous knowledge and attainment. They are using tools developed by others. Intellectual superstar and inventor par excellence, da Vinci was never going to invent the lightbulb because the conceptual and material means weren't there to do it. If Shakespeare were alive today, as people like to say, he would write differently because the English language has changed syntactically, semantically, colloquially. So part of his genius is no longer available for use. People don't expect modern literary geniuses to write in the Elizabethan style. Comparisons just don't work – x does not equal y.

'You could always tell she was a genius'

If you are a genius, rest assured people will talk about you. So one very vague way of measuring the importance of geniuses is to see what others say about them.

The author Henry James said of fellow author Rudyard Kipling that he 'strikes me personally as the most complete man of genius (as distinct from fine intelligence) that I have ever known'. (Ah, those parentheses. James could really do parentheses.) A pretty neat statement for Kipling to cut and paste into his resume.

'Who said what about whom?' quick quiz

1. 'For all his kindness, sociability, and love of humanity, he was nevertheless totally detached from his environment and the human beings included in it.'
   a) Max Born about Albert Einstein
   b) Claude Monet about Titian
   c) Federico García Lorca about George Bernard Shaw

2. 'No, I have not read him – he is far too profound for me.'
   a) Ludwig Wittgenstein about Søren Kierkegaard
   b) John Stuart Mill about David Hume
   c) Arthur Miller about Henry Miller

3. 'Keep an eye on him. One day he will give the world something to talk about.'
   a) Wolfgang Mozart about Ludwig van Beethoven
   b) Robert Greene about William Shakespeare
   c) Henri Matisse about Jackson Pollock

4. 'There was things which he stretched, but mainly he told the truth.'
   a) Huckleberry Finn about Mark Twain
   b) Franklin Roosevelt about Winston Churchill
   c) William Wordsworth about William Blake

The answers, to keep things simple, are all the a)s.

'He changed my life'

'My genius is in my nostrils.' – Friedrich Nietzsche

You might want to measure genius by a number of other criteria more favourable to certain wayward intellects. How did genius X affect the way I live? In what ways do his or her ideas shape our thinking? What contribution did the genius make to humanity's understanding of its place in the universe? And so on. All sorts of measurements spring to mind.

This gives inventors and artists a chance. People like Thomas Edison and Nikola Tesla, even Tim Berners-Lee or Bill Gates have had ideas that have developed into the mechanisms and devices that run the modern world. And this is probably a good thing. People like Johann Sebastian Bach and Mahler and Verdi and even Bob Dylan can reflect and influence the way people think and feel. Yes, so did Hitler and Stalin. But don't think of them in the same way. Bach outlives them with sublime ease.

The truth about philosophers

What exactly is it about philosophers that makes them the top geniuses? To paraphrase Plato: 'What the hell is a philosopher anyway?' Well, they are the original lovers of wisdom – *philos* meaning loving and *sophos* meaning the wise. They get into genius territory early because they are the only game in town.

As an early philosopher you could study anything – maths, science, astronomy, physics. All these words have their origins in Greek words with rather general senses that mean things like 'looking at', 'dividing up', 'thinking about', 'knowing of'. If you did any kind of analytical study in the classical world, you were a philosopher.

And the Greeks' achievement is still with us. If you imagine a philosopher today, chances are he'll be sporting a beard, wearing a toga, and carrying a wax tablet, rather than wearing a corduroy jacket and very square glasses, and not knowing what to do with his bicycle clips.

What is truth?

Philosophers want to know what can be known. So they are like ordinary people in that respect. But most people think they know things and just leave it at that. For the philosopher this is not enough.

The philosopher's launch pad is the Socratic method. This means asking questions about things that you normally don't

PLATO (427–347 BCE) – PHILOSOPHER

- Plato was the founder of the Academy in Athens, where Aristotle was a student. The Academy flourished for over 900 years, from 387 BCE to 529 CE, until it was eventually shut down by Emperor Justinian for being too pagan for the new Christian empire.

- Not too keen on the idea of democracy, Plato instead believed in the rule of philosopher kings.

- The philosopher was originally a wrestler (Plato is a nickname meaning 'broad-shouldered') and a soldier in the Peloponnesian War. After the war he joined the government but fell out with

the Thirty Tyrants. Why? Because they were too tyrannical.

- Plato was a student of Socrates and may have attended his trial. He wrote the Socratic dialogues – Socrates himself wrote nothing. Scholars say the later dialogues become increasingly less Socratic and more Platonic.

- *The Republic* is Plato's key text. Written around 360 B.CE, it sets out his ideas on government, justice and the role of the philosopher.

- Plato certainly had some nutty moments. Like suggesting that Homer should be exiled and his works rewritten.

ask questions about. Questions like 'How do I know I exist?' or 'What is the meaning of justice?' or 'How can I talk about that which cannot be said?' You do need to exercise caution with these kinds of questions; they can cause trouble. To be a successful philosopher you need to be able to get the questions right as much as the answers.

The 21st-century philosopher

Philosophers these days are still university lecturers – much like Plato was. Though now they don't wear togas or even ties, and they sit in lightless common rooms discussing . . . well, the kinds of things they have always discussed. If they're good they might get to tour universities, delivering 'guest lectures', where they become performing artists.

It is hard for philosophers to get the kind of recognition they have historically earned, because our fast-paced, hi-tech, modern societies are quite prepared to bask, pleasured and comforted by the myriad sparkly distractions that rampant capitalist consumerism brings, in philosophical waters so shallow that a toddler could wade in them with little or no concern for its own safety.

The golden days of the professional thinker training up philosopher kings to rule Mediterranean utopias are long gone. A world leader these days is more likely to need a media advisor than a philosopher. Sad but true.

Why I am not a genius

The thing about genius is that you never can tell. By rights I really should have shone through in some exalted field or another. I have an impeccable background, so it's all a bit of a mystery. The signs have always looked pretty auspicious.

I was certainly hot-housed by my father. He employed tutors for me starting when I was only three. As a young child I was given an abacus, a globe, a compass, a geometry set, a chemistry set and a microscope. All of these objects were magical inspiration dust to my fancy. I made the abacus into a truck, used the globe as a bowling ball with test tubes from the chemistry set as pins, used the compass to persuade my little sister that unless her heart always faced north she would die, and used the geometry set and the microscope to carry out some micro-voodoo on her dolls. I was tutored in music by a Miss Anne Dante, who taught me to play cello like Pablo Casals, piano like Vladimir Horowitz, bassoon like Joseph Holbroke and cornet like Bix Beiderbecke. She taught my sister to play harmonica like Sonny Boy Williamson. I always felt she didn't really want us to express ourselves. I was tutored in maths and divinity by Otto O'Brandt, a fiery and troubled Irish-German Catholic-Protestant. Quite a lot of the maths was about probability and we spent a lot of time reading the Racing Post and calculating odds and variables.

At age 14, I was apprenticed to an Italian painter, Tino Bassanini. The first things he taught me were how to drink and visit brothels, but his brushwork was exemplary, and the fact that he was a reckless libertine didn't have much more effect than the occasional six-week absence. The final straw was his failure to appear at my exhibition in Florence, where I showed my best two paintings – *The Day After the Lifting of the Siege of Mafeking* and *The Wreck of the Hesperus II: A Pig's Tale*. I heard later that he could not attend because he was fighting a duel with my father. Whatever happened, Mr. Bassanini was never to reappear and the exhibition was a limited success, so I decided to try academia for a while.

I got into the Sorbonne by becoming a cleaner there. It allowed me to sit in on lots of lectures. After three years or so, aided by a little financial sweetener that Mr. O'Brandt sent from the Cayman Islands, I persuaded a student who was writing a thesis on the modern self to change his name to mine, take some exams and pick up a degree in the comparative study of the social and cultural effects of scientific theory.

Having got my degree from the Sorbonne, I used the same method to pick up a PhD from Harvard in the comparative study of the scientific effects of social and cultural theory. Then I used these degrees to get a job at the CERN Supercollider in Switzerland. I thought doing some physics and working with a particle accelerator would be pretty cool but I joined during a bit of a slow patch – W and Z bosons had already been discovered and the NA48 experiment into Kaon decay was still a few years away – and I never really took to it. I was planning to leave Switzerland anyway as I wanted to try my hand at being a playwright in London.

Of course, being a playwright is not the kind of job that pays much at first. So, my sister, having just snared herself a wealthy industrialist, was looking for some charitable tax relief. O'Brandt put the package together and I had some cash to set me off. I decided that I wanted to start as strongly as possible and so I re-wrote *Hamlet* by William Shakespeare, giving it a bit more of a musical rom-com angle and setting it in Oklahoma. I wanted the soliloquies to be raps, which is undoubtedly what Shakespeare would do if he were writing today, and was pretty pleased (if I do say so myself) with the big solo number, *What's the Question?*, which used some nice phat beats but kept the original iambs '2 bad or not 2 bad, is I or ain't I?' I felt it retained the essence of Shakespeare's play, minus the revenge tragedy bit, but not many theatres wanted to put it on. The part of Hamlet, or Buddy Ham, as I re-titled him, requires an actor of particular sensibilities and the guy I hired turned out to be a psycho. During rehearsal he tried several times to strike me. Reader, I parried him.

While I may go back to exhibiting work in galleries – I recently produced a video installation based on the colour puce for a Madrid gallery – my next project is some mathematical research. O'Brandt and my sister's fourth husband, a government minister, have lined me up a consultancy with the ethical statistical analysis department of a Scottish university. It may well be that another Scottish Enlightenment is about to blossom and that my genius will be recognised at last.

WHO'S WHO IN
HOW TO BE A GENIUS

PENGUIN BOOKS
Published by the Penguin Group
Penguin Group (Australia)
250 Camberwell Road, Camberwell, Victoria 3124, Australia
(a division of Pearson Australia Group Pty Ltd)
This edition is published by Penguin in the following territories: Australia.
All other rights held by Elwin Street.

Other Penguin offices worldwide:
Penguin Group (USA) Inc., 375 Hudson Street, New York, New York 10014, USA
Penguin Group (Canada), 90 Eglinton Avenue East, Suite 700, Toronto,
Canada ON M4P 2Y3 (a division of Pearson Penguin Canada Inc.)
Penguin Books Ltd., 80 Strand, London WC2R 0RL England
Penguin Ireland, 25 St Stephen's Green, Dublin 2, Ireland (a division of
Penguin Books Ltd.)
Penguin Books India Pvt Ltd., 11 Community Centre, Panchsheel Park,
New Delhi 110 017, India
Penguin Group (NZ), 67 Apollo Drive, Rosedale, North Shore 0632, New Zealand
(a division of Pearson New Zealand Ltd.)
Penguin Books (South Africa) (Pty) Ltd., 24 Sturdee Avenue, Rosebank, Johannesburg
2196, South Africa

Penguin Books Ltd, Registered Offices: 80 Strand, London, WC2R 0RL, England

Copyright © 2007 Elwin Street Productions

Conceived and produced by Elwin Street Productions
144 Liverpool Road, London N1 1LA
www.elwinstreet.com

1 3 5 7 9 10 8 6 4 2

Cover design by Adam Laszczuk © Penguin Group (Australia)
Text design by Thomas Keenes
Illustrations by Robin Chevalier
Cover photograph © Bettmann/CORBIS
Printed in China

A CIP catalogue record for this book is available from the National Library of Australia.

ISBN: 978 0 14 300806 4.

penguin.com.au

ON
PURPOSE

WHAT ARE YOU REALLY HERE TO DO?

MAPPING YOUR JOURNEY TO AN EXTRAORDINARY LIFE

STEVE CHAMBERLAIN

Contact the author:
stevechamberlain.co.uk

Cover design by Patrick Fogarty
Illustrations by Patrick Fogarty
Editing by Claire Chamberlain
Typesetting by Helena Traill
Back cover image by Tim Chamberlain

ISBN 978-1-8380025-0-3

For Carol

CONTENTS

PREFACE

'Live as if you were to die tomorrow.
Learn as if you were to live forever.'
Mahatma Gandhi

'Life is an adventure; dare it.'
Mother Theresa

Is your current career path consciously chosen and deeply rewarding?
Are your days defined by a sense of meaning and fulfilment?
Are you creating your life *on purpose*?

If you've been drawn to this book, I'm guessing your answer to one (or maybe even all) of the above questions will be *no*.

Don't worry. If this is indeed the case, you're in good company – not many can truthfully answer *yes* to all. For most of my life, I couldn't either, and through my own journey I've learned first-hand the suffering that results from living without clarity of purpose. I also found that no single book brought together the insights and tools I was looking for; each was a separate fragmented piece of what it takes to create an extraordinary life. This book is designed to bring together each of these pieces in one place.

You're about to take a journey through the seven stages of creating an extraordinary life. You'll begin by finding your values (who you are) and your purpose (what you're here to do). You'll then be given the tools to make this your reality. Along the way, you'll learn how your mind works, discover how you can take every step of this journey in the present moment, and come to realise that everything you've been looking for is already within you.

Each step of the journey has been mapped out *on purpose* and each chapter can be thought of as a distinct stage, leading you deliberately to the next. Therefore, I recommend that you follow the course of this book as you would climb a mountain path: one step at a time.

When we finally complete our journey together, you'll have everything you need to create and lead an extraordinary life: a life led *on purpose*.

My story: A life of quiet ~~desperation~~ inspiration

As a boy growing up in Bristol, England, I witnessed what a life of quiet desperation looks like. Despite what seemed, from the outside, to be a happy, healthy family home, on the inside my mother felt trapped and helpless. She battled daily with a lack of meaning or purpose, as well as a challenging past and negative thought spirals. As a result, she suffered with chronic anxiety and depression, where she would often disappear into her room for hours or days on end in a bid to overcome her inner turmoil. However, despite her determination, including turning to self-help books and therapy, she was unable to overcome either the demons of her past or the sense of despair she felt in the present. She died at the age of 62: a life of quiet desperation had taken its toll.

Throughout my own teenage years and into my late twenties, the patterns my mum had experienced played out for me, too. My life also looked great from the outside: a flat in London, a successful and enviable career, a loving fiancé and exciting holidays. However, my internal experience too was one of quiet desperation. I suffered with the same chronic anxiety and periods of depression, fearing that these were hereditary states I wouldn't be able to escape. This culminated in a series of panic attacks and recurring suicidal thoughts; at one point, I spontaneously quit my well-paid job, certain I was incapable of handling pressure or responsibility.

This is not the life I now lead. ⊃

After navigating my way through my own crisis, I vowed to help others avoid the same fate. Building on my psychology degree, as well as exposure to some of the world's foremost thought leaders, including Malcolm Gladwell, Renée Mauborgne and Sir Ken Robinson[1], I left my events career and completed my coaching qualifications. I had found my purpose: *to help people create and lead extraordinary, enlightened lives.*

I now run my own coaching practice, working with clients ranging from CEOs and Directors, to entrepreneurs and parents. I also have the privilege of working with some of the UK's top emerging talent through my work with Ivy House, helping to bring life-changing learning to the next generation of leaders.

I don't claim to be perfect, and am still making mistakes and learning more every day. Nor do I claim you'll find each of the seven stages easy (you probably won't). But, while everyone's journey is unique, the principles and insights within these pages are applicable to all and the outcome of aligning yourself with them is a life of quiet *inspiration*.

If you're ready to create your life *on purpose*, let's begin…

---

1 While working as an Events Director at London Business Forum.

TESTIMONIALS

The following testimonials come from clients I coached through the seven stages outlined in this book, each after just three months of applying the principles. As with the case studies included throughout, names have been changed to protect client confidentiality, but the testimonials and backgrounds remain unchanged.

'This work has brought clarity, meaning and purpose to my life, and I feel confident to deal with any challenges that might come my way. I feel so much calmer and far less prone to worry or stress. I have a whole new perspective and positive outlook on life.'

Ruth was in her twenties and experiencing recurring challenges with anxiety, depression and low self-esteem. Her father had suffered with alcoholism when she was growing up and, while she had received counselling, she didn't feel she had reached the core of the problem, or achieved her aim of moving past anxiety.

'I've been lucky to meet lots of good coaches in my career. However, none have inspired me enough to make a personal investment in my own development until I met Steve. What Steve has helped me to do, which I feel is unique, is apply learning about myself (my values, beliefs, purpose) to the very practical context of work. I have a clarity I did not have before, which has been transformational for me, resulting in far less stress, comfortable clear decision making and increased performance.'

Clare was a Director of two successful businesses, but struggling to understand which opportunities to pursue, how to turn down business without experiencing anxiety or guilt, and how to balance all of this with the pressures of a young family.

'I can honestly say I get it now. I almost feel like a different person, I am totally comfortable and happy with who I am and have a sense of inner peace. Life actually seems easy!'

Julie had suffered from sexual abuse as a child. When we began working together, she was in her fifties and her adult life until that point had been defined by fear, mistrust and anxiety.

'I was at a stage of my life where I wasn't happy with the direction I was heading in. I lacked any sort of passion or connection to my work and felt like there had to be something more out there for me. Steve has helped me discover my core values and realise I can be whatever I want, if I set my priorities right and take 100 per cent responsibility for my life. I have switched the trajectory of my life by 180 degrees and, for the first time, feel like I'm heading in the right direction.'

Kuba was looking for a way to transition to a career he would be passionate about. He also expressed concerns around a lack of productivity, chaotic thinking and general lack of results when we began working together.

'Subtle shifts in thinking can make a big difference in your life. Steve's approach is innovative, effective and life changing. My biggest insight is that I already had all the answers, but was getting stuck knowing which parts of the puzzle to focus on and which to ignore. I'm more focused, confident, direct and hopeful. I've made concrete, visible changes in my life right across the board, from career, to relationships, to self-care, to future plans.'

Monica was a successful businesswoman working for one of the world's top accountancy firms. However, she had struggled to apply her astute problem-solving skills to her own life, working 60-hour weeks, experiencing strain in her personal relationships and struggling to find peace of mind amidst the chaos.

'I felt an inner conflict – a sense that I did not live my own life; that I had chosen the wrong way. Working with Steve was transformational. I feel I have all the answers now and am happy and free, with the inner confidence to be able to deal with challenges in any situation.'

Anastasia was an HR Consultant and Coach based in Moscow, struggling to balance her business and life as a parent. She worked seven days a week, felt uninspired by her work and was regretful of past decisions.

STAGE ONE
FINDING YOUR COMPASS

Values – who are you, *really*?

*'I wish I'd had the courage to live a life true to myself,
not the life others expected of me.'*
The Top Five Regrets of the Dying, Bronnie Ware

'Be yourself; everyone else is already taken.'
Oscar Wilde

The first vital stage of any journey of note is preparation – making sure you have the map and tools by which to find your way. This is why we begin with values: who you are at the deepest level, and the foundation upon which everything else is built. If you know your core values – captured through words such as growth, drive, compassion or independence – you'll have the compass by which to direct your journey. You'll know which direction to head in, notice when you've strayed off track and understand how to course-correct. Your values are unique to you, and therefore the only instrument by which to guide your direction.

However, values are often misunderstood. We're so used to individuals, companies, governments and even religions acting in ways that are completely out of alignment with their professed values, that we've lost faith in their relevance. How many of us have worked for companies whose practices are in direct contradiction to the values they emblazon on their walls, or seen politicians violating the values their party claims to represent? It's therefore only natural that we've begun to question the relevance of values. We may feel they're just words and have little concept of how they can help us lead a fulfilling life. But that's precisely what they're capable of doing.

What values are *not*

Let's begin the process of identifying your values by first clearing up some common misconceptions.

Values aren't words

Language, while remarkable, is at its deepest level imperfect, as a word can only ever be a pointer or a symbol for the subject at hand. For example, the word *mountain* is not a mountain; it's a symbolic representation of a mountain. If you were to trek through a landscape made entirely of the word 'mountain', written thousands of times in different heights, fonts and colours, your experience would be fundamentally different to that of hiking through a real mountain range. To a toddler who hasn't yet learned to read, this word is simply seen as eight meaningless squiggles on a page. A mountain is infinitely more complex than any one word or series of words can possibly portray.

The same goes for values. The word *integrity* is just a symbol. What it points to is infinitely more complex, rich and meaningful than words or images could possibly convey. How would you describe integrity in a sentence? How would you draw it? Would your representation ring true for everyone, or does integrity mean different things to different people?

Understanding your values, then, is not about simply picking desirable words, but rather choosing the symbol that most closely points to who you are at the deepest level.

Values aren't positive attributes

It's easy to assume that, when identifying your values, you should choose attributes or traits that you perceive as positive. This may lead you to choose value words such as *contribution*, *kindness* or *freedom* over *winning*, *security* or *control*, which can have more negative associations. However, you can drop all labels of 'good' or 'bad' here; in the world of values, *control* is no more or less positive than *contribution*; it's simply a case of which is true for you.

To help illustrate, we may feel hesitant in selecting *winning* as a value. However, some of our most inspirational role models, including Roger Federer and Rafael Nadal, embody this value in a positive way, thereby inspiring others to fulfil their own potential.

Values aren't a choice

You don't choose your values. A common mistake when looking to identify values is to print out a list of value words and approach them as if selecting off an *à la carte* menu. This inevitably leads to bias, as we opt for words that we see as worthy or advantageous. However, we can no more pick our values than we can choose our height or eye colour. They point to who we already are in our essence, and what we hold dear, not who we wish ourselves to be.

Values aren't priorities

Values are often discussed in much the same way we might talk about priorities, or what's important to us at any given moment. 'What do you prioritise at this point in your life, and how might that change when you get older?' could easily be substituted for 'What do you value at this point in your life, and how might that change when you get older?' This is perfectly valid, but it's not how we're using the word 'value' here. Values, as we're talking about them, go far beyond priorities. We're using the word to depict something much deeper. They're the words or pointers that best describe what makes you unique. What is it, at a fundamental level, that sets you apart from your siblings, friends or peers?

What values *are*

Values are the words that best describe who you are and what matters to you most at the deepest level. Put simply, values – and more specifically, core values – point to who you are in your essence. The use of the term 'core' implies that they run through the very centre of your being. Your unique fingerprint of values is part of what makes you unique from every other human on the planet, despite sharing 99.9 per cent of the same DNA.[2] They determine what's most important to you, what needs to be honoured and what you won't accept, and therefore help to guide and shape your actions and experiences throughout your life. When you understand your values, you understand who you are at the deepest level and what choices will serve you. However, many of us are only partially aware of what our values are, and even fewer actively use them as a compass by which to guide our lives. Yet this is exactly what they are capable of doing.

Living without understanding your values is like beginning a journey without a compass. You won't know which direction to head in and will likely find yourself beset by indecision at every turn. There's little consistency to your choices, and a decision taking you in one direction today might be followed by a subsequent decision taking you in the opposite direction tomorrow. You could be left feeling overwhelmed and unable to move forwards. This is how many of us live our lives – but it doesn't have to be that way. Knowing your values will provide you with the compass to guide your actions. There can be

---

2 Based on DNA research led by Professor Marcus Feldman, Stanford University, 2002.

no more important step in creating a fulfilling life than to understand and align with your values.

A values-driven life

A values-driven life is defined by clarity and integrity. You have crystal clarity on who you are and what's important to you. And you have the integrity that comes with aligning every action and decision with this awareness. A life aligned with your core values is defined by a sense of flow, where a dynamic, creative energy infuses every action, and life is experienced as an unfolding adventure in which you're a co-creator.

Ralph Waldo Emerson's much quoted line, 'Life is a journey, not a destination,' points to a values-driven life. The landmark you're heading for is not a destination to arrive at, where all your toil and hard work is finally rewarded by an easy life. Rather, when aligned with your values, the journey towards your goal becomes intrinsically rewarding in and of itself. Toil and struggle is simply a sign that you're off-track and need to course-correct. Once you reach your intended goal, you're then compelled to continue on to new challenges over the horizon. Your values give you a direction of travel, not an end destination, and you begin to understand on a deep level that fulfilment is the result of experiencing, growing, evolving and exploring, rather than *arriving*. By continuously moving in the direction of your values, your life will become an outer representation of your inner values, and there will be a congruency to everything you do. A truly fulfilling life will always be values-driven, and a values-driven life will always be truly fulfilling.

The alternative

The alternative to a values-driven life is, sadly, the one that you might be more familiar with. You may experience a lack of clarity on who you are and what you're here to achieve. You might feel a background sense of discontent, but are unsure why or how to course-correct. In many ways it feels like a rudderless life, where you 'fall into' jobs and end up playing roles that don't serve you or those around you. You may find motivation a struggle and often procrastinate, or end up doing things you feel you *should* be doing. Tragically, this can often lead to you believing there's something wrong with *you*.

You may also typically struggle to make decisions, particularly the major ones in your life:

'What should I do in this situation?'
'Which job offer should I accept?'
'Is this a relationship I really want to invest in?'

These are the kind of broad questions you might ask yourself when you don't know your values. And the answers you will get from such imprecise questions will be predictably vague:

'Maybe I should do this? Or I could do that? I don't know.'
'This career is more financially rewarding, but the other would give me more time with my family; I'm not sure which is the best option.'
'I do like them, but we're starting to argue a bit. Maybe I should cut my losses now... but what if this is a pattern I need to break?'

This type of circular thinking can play out endlessly if you don't know your values.

A key realisation here is that your mind is an incredible tool for storing and retrieving information, but *not* for making decisions (something we'll come to when we explore mindset). Without knowing your values, you have nothing reliable by which to guide your choices or your direction of travel.

Being unaware of your values can also leave you open to fear, anxiety, guilt and a range of other unhealthy emotions, because any time you're out of sync with them, you will suffer. Whether this is felt as a background sense of unease, a sudden dose of guilt, or the paralysis of depression depends upon the extent to which your actions have compromised your values. For example, it's likely in the past you've experienced taking an action that you instantly regretted – one that left you with a heavy feeling in your stomach and had you wishing you could go back and make a different choice. To experience this, you can be sure you've violated a core value. In addition, the low-level dissatisfaction many of us experience in life also has its roots in values. For example, if you value *creativity*, you'll suffer if given a work project that involves endless detail and spreadsheets; if you value *control*, you'll suffer when a project has lots of moving parts that you can't directly influence; and if you value *growth*, you'll suffer in roles where there's no opportunity to develop or progress.

The values principle

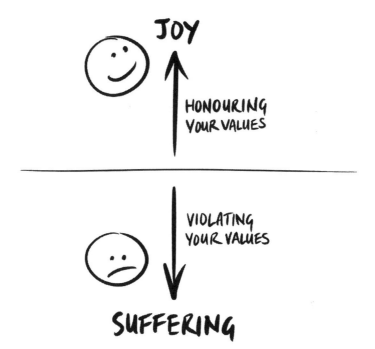

Suffering follows the violation of your values *every time*, and the level of suffering you experience is determined by the extent to which you're out of alignment. This unerring consistency points to what I call the *Values Principle* which, like all laws of nature, plays out without exception. This is a key realisation as you look to create a fulfilling life. It also means that, while unpleasant, suffering serves an important purpose.

If you were asked, 'Do you want to suffer?' your answer would naturally be: 'No.' This natural response may lead you to think of suffering as a form of adversary that must be avoided or overcome. However, what if suffering served a purpose, providing valuable information to help guide your journey? If that were true, then rather than turning your back or doing battle, you might choose to accept your present suffering and ask, 'What is the lesson here?' or 'Where have I lost my way?' Instead, we typically close ourselves off to our suffering by denying it, perhaps by drinking or medicating ourselves to numb the pain, or maybe by losing ourselves in escapes, such as box sets or gaming. But avoiding your suffering stops you from realising which value you've compromised, and therefore how you can course-correct going forwards.

While nobody wants to suffer, the *Values Principle* determines that much unnecessary suffering will drop away as soon as you realign your life around your core values[3]. This principle, therefore, is one of the keys to your freedom from suffering.

---

3 Holding limiting beliefs, and resisting reality are two other key sources of unnecessary suffering; areas we'll address later in our journey, when we come to beliefs and mindfulness.

When I violated my core values

At 28, I quit my job as the Events Director of a leading London events company, to get away from the stress and anxiety I perceived this role to be causing me. At the time I didn't know what values were, let alone my unique core values or the extent to which I would suffer if I compromised them. I was about to learn the hard way! Unbeknown to me, by stepping away from a challenging yet inspiring career, I had just violated my core value of *growth* – and the suffering arrived instantly.

I remember meeting my dad for a walk around Hampstead Heath a few days after handing in my notice. My world had changed, but not in the way I'd hoped. Prior to handing in my notice, I was convinced the weight of the world would drop from my shoulders, and I'd feel happy and free; this turned out to be far from reality. Within a few short days I looked and felt like a broken person. My body language had perceptibly changed, I felt lethargic and walked with my head down. I muttered abrupt responses to my dad's questions and felt a strange sense of disconnection from the world. I had a heavy feeling in my gut – a sense I'd violated something important and made a terrible mistake, but felt powerless to do anything about it. I didn't know it at the time, but my actions had brought about the onset of depression.

Rather than finding myself magically gifted a dream job that would solve all my problems (a fantasy that I can now look back on with the humour that comes with perspective!), I instead began applying for jobs I wanted less that the one I'd just left, in order to pay the bills. And so I found myself in a job interview for a charity, lying about my selfless decision to leave the corporate world in order to work for their cause. I was now unconsciously violating my number one core value of *integrity*, and the suffering cranked up to a whole new level. I accepted the subsequent job offer and began a period of my career where I suffered daily with anxiety, alongside periodic bouts of depression and suicidal thoughts. I was out of integrity in my career, and I wouldn't move beyond my suffering until that changed; a process that would take me several years.

The suffering (anxiety and depression) I experienced can be compared to the pain that results from touching a hot stove. While I would never have chosen this pain, it served a vital purpose, telling me in no uncertain terms not to repeat this action again. It was through this experience that I came to know my core values of *integrity*, *growth*, *family*, *meaning* and *excellence*, which later compelled me to take the leap ↩

of setting up my own coaching practice, despite having a mortgage, two young children and only a small amount of savings. I knew on a deep level that suffering had served its purpose: it had shown me powerfully where I was off track so I could take a different path. I now look back on this experience as a vital part of my personal journey, which has allowed me to create a genuinely fulfilling life, and enabled me to help others to do the same. I personally wouldn't change a thing, but this suffering is avoidable if you can learn to understand and honour your values.

How to identify your values

If you're unsure what your values are, how can you best uncover them? Many people start with a list of values words, but this can (and often will) lead you to select values you deem as desirable, and to reject any you perceive as less worthy. As we learned earlier, values exist beyond the poles of 'good' and 'bad', so you're aiming to uncover what or who you *already are* in your essence, rather than values you admire.

So, how do you identify your core values? By shining a spotlight onto your life. When have you experienced profound feelings of joy, contentment, fulfilment and flow? Look for the value you were fulfilling there. When have you felt angry, discontented, unfulfilled or stuck? Look for the value you were violating. For example, did you experience a sense of joy and a burst of positive energy when you quit your office admin job at the age of 20 to go travelling? If so, *adventure* or *freedom* may be among your core values. On the flip side of the same example, did you experience lethargy and frustration when you stayed in a repetitive full-time job? Again, this may point to values of *adventure* or *freedom*, but this time through compromising, rather than honouring, these values. You know you've found a core value when it has played out many times over the course of your lifetime, always with strong associated emotions. Let's begin the process of uncovering your values…

Four steps to uncovering your core values

Finding your values is like playing detective. The clues will all be there, as you will have brought your values into every interaction, job, relationship and situation you've ever been in. They're inseparable from who you are, and have therefore already played out, whether you've been conscious of them or not: now it's about bringing them to the surface. There are four key steps you'll follow to do so: *FEEL* (*Finding* your long-list of values; *Establishing* which of these are your core values; *Explaining* what they mean to you; and *Listing* them by order of priority). Your feelings will be your guide.

Uncovering your values

Step one: find your long-list of potential values

Your first step is to identify a long-list of values that you feel are potentially important to you. As explained earlier, rather than looking for priorities, which naturally ebb and flow over time, you're looking for your deepest values, which are timeless. You'll know if something is a possible core value if it plays out in all areas of your life and is consistent from a young age right through until the present day. For example, if you value *justice*, then times when you felt there was an injustice at school will have affected you much more strongly than your peers, and this will still play out for you in your workplace today. You'll also likely be strongly affected by instances of injustice in your relationships, as well as in wider society.

Let's begin the process of building your long-list, by creating a timeline of your peak and trough moments: ⮌

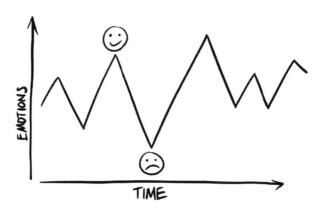

a. Take a blank sheet of paper and, starting from your earliest memories to the left of the page and then moving to the right towards the present day, mark any key peak and trough experiences that stand out in your life. For the peaks, you're looking for times when you experienced great flow, energy, peace or joy; those for which you have a vivid positive memory, as if your mind took a snapshot. Some of these might be significant life events, such as passing your driving test, securing a job promotion or getting married. Others could be less obvious events that hold real meaning for you, such as a particular family gathering, a moment on a holiday or a time you thrived at work. For the troughs, you're looking for times where you suffered, experienced toxic emotions such as anger, or felt a strong sense of disconnection. Some of these might be significant life events, such as failing an exam, a long-term relationship break-up or being made redundant. Others could be less obvious, such as a point in your career when your energy and motivation hit rock bottom, a time when a friend's actions triggered you, or any other experience that still brings up strong negative emotions. The only exception here is an event where you would expect anyone to suffer, such as the death of a loved one, where a core value may not be at play. Continue this process until you've captured all the key high and low points from your life.

b. When your timeline is complete, take each of the peak experiences one at a time. Tune fully into the memory and associated emotions, and consider the following questions:

- What was the key factor that created the sense of joy, contentment, fulfilment or flow? (For example, if a holiday where you experienced peak states while taking part in a series of adrenaline-fuelled activities came to mind, you may value *courage*, *excitement* or *achievement*.)
- If you could take one thing from that situation and bring it into the rest of your life, to help you experience these peak states more often, what would it be? (For example, if an evening came to mind where you and a couple of close friends had time to connect on a deep level, *connection*, *love* or *friendship* might be your value.)

c. Repeat this process for each of the peak memories in your life, adding all the potential value words you've identified to your long-list.

d. Next, consider your trough experiences. Again, taking one at a time, tune fully into the memory and associated emotions, and ask yourself the following questions:

- What was the key factor that created the suffering? (For example, was it that you, or someone else, lied? In which case the value could be *honesty*, *truth* or *integrity*.)
- If you could have changed one thing about the situation, which would have taken away the suffering, what would that be? (For example, if you wish you'd stepped up and taken the lead, rather than staying in the background, *leadership* or *drive* could be a value.) ↩

e.　Repeat this process until you have a long-list of potential values, likely to be somewhere between 15 and 30, but fewer or more is absolutely fine. You may find that some of the words are similar to others on your list, which is to be expected at this stage.

Step two: Establish your core values

We've deliberately avoided referring to a values list until this point, to ensure you uncover your authentic values. However, this is the perfect time to scan and see if any additional value words resonate for you and should be included in your long-list. You can download a sample values list for free at *stevechamberlain.co.uk/livingonpurpose*.

Now it's time to find which of the value words on your long-list are your *core* values:

a.　First, take your long-list and read each word in turn. Any words that no longer resonate for you can be removed from the list, by striking a line through them. This isn't to say that these secondary values are no longer important and should be ignored, but they're not the biggest players for you and therefore won't be the best ones to steer your major life decisions by.

b.　Now go through your list again, this time looking for the value words that resonate most strongly for you. Star those you feel point to something that has always been important to you and always will be. Your goal is to get a short-list of four to seven value words[4] that are the big players for you, but initially you may find yourself starring ten or more words, which is a natural part of this process.

4　This isn't prescriptive, but tends to be the optimal number. Any fewer and you may not have sufficient self-knowledge to guide your decisions. Any more, and you may find the clarity that comes from knowing your core values is diluted.

c. Now consider whether any of the values are interrelated. For example, if you've starred both *peace* and *calmness* are these two separate values, or do they form part of the same picture for you? If they are related, which word resonates most strongly for you? Keep the star for this one and delete from the other. If you still have more than seven values starred after this process, read your short-list again and ask yourself which values aren't quite as important to you as the others. You can then remove these stars. Repeat this process until you have four to seven core values identified.

d. Leave any remaining words that haven't been starred or crossed out. These will come into play in the next step.

Step three: Explain what each value means to you

This step gives you a deeper understanding of your core values. This is important, because the same word points to something different for everyone. For example, the value *charity* may conjure images of working on the front-line in a war-torn conflict zone for some, while for others it brings to mind offering help and support to those in the local community. Both are equally valid, but understanding what your values represent for *you* will help ensure you steer your course correctly. This is done by attributing two additional words to each of your core values. ↩

Imagine the core value word – in the above example *charity* – as being engraved on a signpost[5] a few yards in front of you. Your goal is to find two associated words that laser the direction of the signpost directly at *you*. For example, the person who views *charity* within a frontline context may add the two associated value words *commitment* and *courage,* so their signpost reads CHARITY | *commitment* | *courage*. Alternatively, the person who views *charity* within a more local setting may have CHARITY | *community* | *contribution*. This distinction will lead to very different life choices.

Let's do this process for your core values now:

a.   Start by writing out your core values – those still starred from the previous exercise – on a blank sheet of paper.

b.   Now come back to any remaining value words from your original list that weren't crossed out. Take each word at a time and consider whether it might form part of one of your core values. For example, *achievement* and *performance* may come together with a core value of *excellence*, while *wisdom* and *spirituality* may come together with *meaning*.

c.   Finally, review your latest values list to make sure that each core value has the word that most resonates first, and then two associated words that define what that value means to you (for example, TRUST / *integrity* / *honesty*).

Step four: List your values in order of priority

This final step may seem a strange one. Surely knowing your core values is enough? Why the need to order them? The answer lies in the complexity of our lives. There will be many instances where you can't honour all of your values equally,

---

5 I was introduced to this tool by a colleague a number of years back, and have included here as my clients find this invaluable.

resulting in a natural tension between them. For example, you may have a core value of *freedom* and another of *connection*. You're at a crossroads in your career, and the opportunity to work for yourself arises. This possibility excites you, but you also know that in doing so you'll no longer work as part of a team. Your decision may depend on whether *freedom* or *connection* is higher on your list. Again, there is no right or wrong decision as determined by some external judgement, but rather an internal sense of knowing what is right for you, given your core values.

Let's order your values:

a.   To begin, simply see if you find it an easy process to order your values from one (as your most important value), and then sequentially down.

b.   If you feel unclear on how to order your core values, look back over your life and search for patterns that have played out. Which values have tended to be the biggest players for you? Which have led to the strongest positive or negative emotions when you have honoured, compromised or violated them? Which value has always been front of mind when you've had to take big decisions?

c.   If you're still unclear, project forwards by asking which of your core values would be most important to you in shaping a major upcoming life decision, such as a new career or house move.

When you've finished ordering your values, add them to the Purpose Primer, which can be downloaded for free at *stevechamberlain.co.uk/livingonpurpose*. We'll come back to this on the next stage of our journey.

Client case study – Anastasia

Anastasia was exhausted, demotivated and on the verge of a breakdown when we began working together. She was working eighty-hour weeks, including evenings and weekends, and was often in tears as she talked about how little time she spent with her daughter, who was just six at the time. She knew her life was out of alignment, but had no idea how to course-correct. To help her do so, we uncovered and ordered her values, which were: 1. *Transparency*; 2. *Family*; 3. *Freedom*; 4. *Success*; 5. *Evolution*. Through this process, Anastasia had a key insight: she had chased *success* above all else, just as her father had while she was growing up, but she now realised that this value had always been less important to her than *transparency*, *family* and *freedom*. Success may have been her father's number one value, but it wasn't hers. Now, with a daughter of her own, tirelessly chasing success at work meant violating her more important value of *family*, resulting in the stress she had been experiencing.

Anastasia also realised that an organisation she sourced some of her work from was violating her number one value of *transparency* by deliberately misleading clients, which had been a source of internal conflict for her. Anastasia therefore chose to step back from this work. The moment she took this decision, a weight lifted off her shoulders. She had agonised over this situation for months, but now that she could make a clear, values-led decision, it was easy to act. This choice freed up significant time for her family and gave her the freedom to take on work with more values-aligned companies.

Anastasia's final insight was that she had always assumed success was limited to the workplace but, at this moment in time, helping to create a loving family environment was a key part of what success meant to her. This enabled her to find an optimal work/life balance, while still honouring her value of *success*.

When we spoke again a couple of months after implementing these changes, Anastasia was glowing, talking proudly about the work projects she'd been able to take on, and the time she had carved out for her husband and daughter. Knowing the order of her values had given her the clarity by which to course-correct.

Simply being conscious of your values will have a significant positive impact in your life. You'll start to understand why you enjoy what you enjoy, which situations you need to avoid, and how you can cultivate more positive experiences and emotions. But that's just the beginning…

How to live according to your values

Now you're conscious of your core values, you'll likely find yourself naturally drawn to honouring them in your life, but you can take control of, and accelerate, this process by consciously using your values to guide *every* decision you take. For example, you can get into the habit of asking, 'What action here would best honour my value of [insert core value]?' The more you do this, the more your life will become a reflection of who you are and what you stand for.

Realigning your life around your values

Step one: Find where you're currently out of alignment with your values

The first step is to ask where your energy levels are low, and where you are currently struggling or suffering in your life. For example, you may find a particular relationship, work project or role draining. Jot down each specific situation that comes to mind in the table below. Next, look at your core values list and identify which value(s) you're currently out of alignment with in each of the situations. For example, is your marriage lacking *fairness* because you feel the relationship is unbalanced? Is a work project making you feel disconnected, because it involves you working alone rather than in *collaboration?* Or is the job itself no longer honouring your core value of *growth,* because there are no development or promotion opportunities?

Challenging situation	Value(s) being compromised

You'll know your list is complete when you can confidently say that, if all those areas were resolved, your life would be defined by energy and flow.

Step two: Determine how to realign

Now use the tool below to explore how you could realign each situation with your core values. For example, in your marriage, you may decide that you could honour *fairness* by 1) speaking to your partner about how you're feeling; 2) offering some possible solutions on how to bring the relationship back into balance; or 3) drawing up a personal weekly planner that includes activities you know will re-energise you.

- Challenging situation:

- Core value(s) it's out of alignment with:

- What three steps could you take to realign this situation with your values?

    1.
    2.
    3.

- Of the options identified, which aligns most closely with your core values?

- If you took this course of action, would it sit well with you, regardless of outcome?

- Do you choose to take this course of action? If *yes*, move to step three. If *no*, repeat this process until you find a values-aligned course of action you're happy to take. ↪

Step three: Create an action plan

Now you've chosen your course of action, it's time to make that your reality. The key to this step is considering when, where and how to take action, to achieve the best possible outcome. For example, raising your relationship concerns with your partner when you're both tired, without preparing what you plan to say, is unlikely to set you up for success. Instead, choosing a time when you're both refreshed will likely play out much better. You'll also find that focusing on concrete examples ('When you texted me to say you were staying out with your work friends, it meant I had to rearrange my plans and I felt really frustrated') rather than subjective sweeping statements ('You keep on messing me around') will help. The steps below can be used to map this out.

- What is my desired outcome?
- When and where do I choose to take action?
- What preparation can I do to help ensure the best outcome for all?

How to use your values to make decisions

Values-led choices take you *precisely* where you want to go, saving you the lost time and suffering that results from straying off-track. Now you are conscious of your values, you're able to use them to ask higher-quality questions to determine your ideal path.

Client case study – Clare

Clare was a Director of two thriving companies, a loving wife and mother to two young children. When we began working together, she was experiencing overload, pulled between different work projects and unable to carve out quality time with her family. She had no clear criteria by which to decide which opportunities to take on, and didn't feel able to say no, for fear of letting people down and experiencing the resulting guilt.

We identified Clare's values – 1. *Love*; 2. *Approval*; 3. *Responsibility*; 4. *Efficiency*; and 5. *Security* – and then viewed her current situation through this lens. She realised only certain projects fulfilled her top three core values, and that those she didn't *love*, have the opportunity to take full *responsibility* for, or receive *approval* from an end beneficiary for, could easily be delegated to others. She had previously assumed *security* was her highest priority and had equated this with taking on every project, for fear the jobs or money might run out. However, realising this was leading her to feel overwhelmed, she was free to prioritise her top core values when taking future decisions.

In our next session together, Clare was buzzing, saying that for the first time, she had been able to make a clear choice between work projects based upon her values, and was then able to communicate which ones she was no longer able to take on. Others within the company then benefited, by being given opportunities that wouldn't have otherwise come ↩

their way. I saw Clare again some months later and she now only works on values-aligned projects, has a bigger impact within her companies and experiences no guilt when turning down opportunities that don't align with her values.

Here are the four steps to taking values-based decisions:

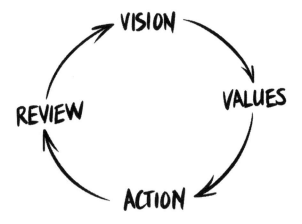

Step one – envision your ideal outcome

The first step is to know where you are headed. The following questions will serve you when you reach a decision point:

- Knowing my core values are [insert core values], what is my ideal outcome?
- What would be the best possible outcome for all involved?
- If *anything* was possible, what would I love to achieve here?

For example, imagine you're feeling demotivated in your current job, having worked in the same position for the past five years. When you started at the company, you loved coming to work, but now you're watching the clock each day. Your core values, in order of importance, are **growth**, **leadership**, **success**, **integrity** and **family**. The above questions might lead you to identify the following goal:

To step up to my first management position, build a team that I'm proud of, increase my salary and begin to look forward to work again.

Step two – come back to your values

Use your values to decide on the best course of action. The following questions can be used to guide this process:

- How can I best honour my core values of [insert core values] to achieve my desired outcome?
- Which are my top three core values, and how can I align with them here?
- Does this approach sit well with me? (Tune into your body here to gauge whether your chosen action is truly values aligned. You'll feel it in your gut if it's not quite right, in which case revisit the questions above).

Continuing our earlier example, these questions might lead to the following insights and plan of action:

'Growth, leadership and success are my top core values, so I can see why this period of my career has been so challenging. I've been coming home miserable for the past year, and realigning around these values will help me be my old self again for my loved ones (**family**). However, the same value also means that I don't want to end up in a role that requires me to work evenings or weekends.'

'I believe in the goals my team is trying to achieve (**integrity**), so I'm keen to explore how I might be able to step up to a management role within my company. I get on well with my manager, so trust that having an open and honest conversation with her is the best approach (**integrity**). I am confident I could add significant value by leading a development team in our area of the business (**success**). Therefore, in preparation for speaking with my manager, I will create a business case outlining the key benefits.'

'If, on the back of our conversation, it's clear there are no opportunities to step up within my current area, I'll ask to explore opportunities to take on a secondment to a management role (**leadership**) elsewhere within the business, and line management training (**growth**).'

'If there are no opportunities for me to develop within the next 12 months, then I'll choose to explore opportunities elsewhere. In that instance, I will still give my best for the remainder of my time here (**integrity**) and will search for companies and roles that align with my values.'

Step three – take action

Make it happen. If now is the optimal time, do it. If not, diarise it. If you need to put in some preparation time, get started. In the above example, this would mean setting aside time to create a business case, as well as preparing for the meeting. By making commitments and sticking to them in this way, your life will inevitably become an outer reflection of your values.

Step four – review and course-correct

After the event, you can reflect on whether you achieved the desired outcome and honoured your values as planned. If not, this is valuable information. Instead of beating yourself up, use this as a learning experience. The below questions can support this process:

- What lessons have I learned?
- What would I do differently next time, given the information I now have?
- What have I learned about my values and how I can best honour them moving forwards?

Bringing it all together

It's important to understand that knowing your values doesn't take away the complexity or challenge of life. However, on a deep level, you'll become clear on who you are, what you stand for and what needs to be done. By anchoring your actions to your values, there will be an integrity and consistency to your choices that, over time, will transform your life.

Understanding your values also gives you the compass by which to find the unique contribution you're here to make. Which leads us to the next stage on our journey: purpose.

Reflection

- Where are you currently suffering in your life? Which core value(s) are you out of alignment with?
- What simple steps could you take to realign with your values, thereby regaining direction and balance?
- What's your key insight from this stage of your journey, and what will you do differently as a result?

STAGE TWO

MAPPING YOUR DESTINATION

Purpose – what are you *really* here to do?

'Having an exciting destination is like setting a needle
in your compass. From then on, the compass knows
only one point – its ideal. And it will faithfully guide you
there through the darkest nights and fiercest storms.'
Daniel Boone, American pioneer, explorer and folk hero

'When you are inspired by some great purpose...
dormant forces, faculties and talents become alive
and you discover yourself to be a greater person than
you ever dreamed yourself to be.'
Patanjali, Hindu author, mystic and philosopher

Now you know your values, you have the compass by which to inform your direction of travel. However, it's crucial that you also know where you are headed, for a life without purpose is like a journey without a destination.

A meaningful and fulfilling life is the natural result of purposeful living. A sense of meaning comes from knowing why you are here, and fulfilment comes through, literally, fulfilling this purpose. You may previously have tried to find fulfilment or meaning through your career, financial or other achievements, but unless such goals have been aligned with your purpose, you'll have found your search coming up short.

The question 'What are you here to do?' can have many answers. You might say to pay the bills and provide for your family; to have a rewarding career; to be a good parent; and so on. However, the same question could also be answered on a much deeper level. Implicit within it is the suggestion that you have a purpose that is unique only to you. Something you may or may not have discovered at this point in your life, but that is your calling – your opportunity to add unique value to the world.

Finding your purpose, then, is a crucial step on your journey.

A life without purpose

Unfortunately, many of us find ourselves leading lives without a true sense of purpose. We only need to sit on a commuter train on a Monday morning to experience the discontent that's endemic in our modern society. Companies are demanding more and more of us, with the old nine-to-five jobs all but gone and replaced by working weeks that can see these hours doubled. Many companies exist with the primary objective of making money for their shareholders, and working long hours in the service of this can be draining, demoralising and stress-inducing.

You may believe the reason for staying in a job or career that doesn't fulfil you is the security it offers. You need a regular paycheck, healthcare benefits and a pension scheme to provide for your family and prepare for future retirement, right? This is a logical argument and there's absolutely no problem with choosing a job or career that provides benefits and financial security, as long as you *love* what you're doing. However, most of us will be working until we're at least 65 and are likely to find ourselves spending longer in the office than we do at home for much of this time. Therefore, to choose workplace benefits over doing a job that you love simply isn't a fair pay-off.

The negative consequences of chronic stress on our health and relationships are well documented. By doing a job you don't enjoy for a lifetime, you're actually damaging your chances of enjoying that retirement package you've been slaving for, and your habits will have been set. After all, a career underpinned by frustration and discontent doesn't set the road map for a retirement filled with freedom and joy. So, if you want to have fun in retirement, have fun in your role *now*. If you want to enjoy freedom when you no longer work, find freedom in your work *now*. In this way, you choose to *be* what you want to experience and drop the illusion that tomorrow will be anything other than what you set in motion today.

Purpose doesn't apply to the workplace alone. Far from it! Finding the contribution you're here to make as an individual, within your community, as a parent or in retirement can lead to a profound sense of meaning. Is there purpose behind your everyday actions, or are you just trying to get through the seemingly endless chores and responsibilities that come with life?

A purposeful life

Many of us won't have known there was a purpose to uncover, so have yet to even contemplate what it might be. Even if we have contemplated this subject, or have been trying to find the 'right' career, we may have unwittingly asked the *wrong* questions; those that don't take us towards a fulfilling and contented life. The good news is that discovering your purpose isn't as difficult as you may believe; it's all about the quality of your questions.

The wrong questions

'What career should someone like me choose?'
This question anchors you in the past. If you come from a financially impoverished family, then this question might lead you to decide that

further education or particular career paths aren't for you. It can also limit your perceived choices even if you come from a more financially advantaged background. For example, you may feel you *have* to go to university or *should* follow your parents' career paths, even if this doesn't align with your strengths or passions.

The way this question is worded also implies there's only one right path to take. *Should* can helpfully be replaced with *could*, and instantly the burden falls away. 'I *could* be a doctor' or 'I *could* work for a charity' carries a very different energy to 'I *should* be a doctor' or 'I *should* work for a charity'. You don't *have* to do anything.

'Which career path makes the most money?'

The extent to which this is a good question depends upon your desired outcome. If you're judging the success of your life by the size of your bank account, then this is a logical question, leading you in the direction of higher salaries and lucrative bonus schemes.

If, on the other hand, you're judging success by how fulfilled or happy you are, this question no longer serves you. This is because the underlying assumption that money buys happiness has been proven to be unfounded. Once our income reaches a level where we're able to comfortably pay our bills and achieve a certain level of financial freedom ($75,000 in the US[6]), subsequent wage increases have virtually no impact upon our long-term happiness. We'll look at the reasons behind this surprising finding in the final stage of our journey.

Conversely, it's also important to clarify here that a purposeful life is not, by definition, a poor one. We only need to look at the bank accounts of Oprah Winfrey or JK Rowling to know that a life built upon our unique offering can bring with it incredible financial rewards. However, in such instances, financial wealth is the *result* of the contribution we're making and not the *purpose* of it. If we pursue money for its own end, while our bank balance may be overflowing, on the inside we'll still experience a sense of lack if we're out of alignment with our values and purpose.

'Which career sounds impressive?'

This is the question your ego (your self-concept) wants to ask: 'What sounds impressive if I'm being introduced at a dinner party?' There's nothing wrong with a job title that sounds impressive or that sparks interest in other people, as long as it sparks genuine passion in you, too. If not, you'll likely experience 'imposter syndrome': a feeling that you're out of integrity and in danger of being 'found out'.

'What do my parents/significant others think I should do?'
This question implies that your parents, or significant others, know what's right for you better than you do. They don't. Not because they don't mean well, but because it's simply not possible for them to know you better than you know yourself. If they value *security* but you value *freedom,* then the advice they give in good faith won't be in your best interest. In an ideal world, the role of our significant others would be to ask us the kind of questions that help us find our own path. However, they're unlikely to know which questions to ask, or the framework within which they fit. Let's come onto this now, by providing both, so you can start the journey to finding your own purpose.

Five steps to finding purpose

There are five sequential steps to finding your purpose and the good news is that you've already completed step one, by uncovering your values:

- Step one – identify your values
- Step two – identify your strengths
- Step three – identify your passions
- Step four – find your element
- Step five – find your purpose

Let's go through steps two to five in detail together now, pausing at each stage to ask the *right* questions – those that will guide you to a fulfilling and contented life.

Step two – identify your strengths

You might not think you have many – or any! – strengths.

Everyone has strengths.

As I heard it eloquently put recently, we're all gifted, it's just that many of us never look inside the box. We may be good at driving; cooking; listening; learning; teaching; drawing; swimming; selling; organising… the list goes on.

Understanding your strengths is a crucial step on the way to finding your purpose. By utilising these strengths, you'll be able to fulfil your potential and add your own unique value to the world.

We tend to excel at what we love and love what we excel at. When our career aligns with our innate talents, we achieve true security – the security of being irreplaceable in our field. Our employer is no longer our source of security; our *strengths* are. So, where do your natural talents lie? What are you so good at that you take it for granted?

Identifying your strengths

Take a few minutes to make a list of your innate strengths, no matter how obscure or insignificant they may seem at this stage. If you're unsure, or want some help, visit *stevechamberlain.co.uk/livingonpurpose* to download a free Strengths Surfacing tool designed to support you.

Step three – identify your passions

To choose to spend your time doing anything other than what you love will leave you feeling unfulfilled. Therefore, the next step in discovering your purpose is to get back in touch with your passions.

What do you love to do? If you relish solving problems, there will be careers, volunteering opportunities and hobbies that are crying out for your skillset. If you love numbers, words, music, dance, science, mechanics, woodwork, crafting or anything else, the same will be true.

Which subject could you talk about for hours? Which topic could you read up on that wouldn't feel like homework? What work would feel more like play? What will you still choose to do after you've retired?

Identifying your passions

Take a few minutes to make a list of your passions, using these additional prompt questions where helpful:

- What are your current hobbies and interests? What did you love to do in your spare time as a child? What type of books, audios and videos are you naturally drawn to? What would you love to do more of, and what activities couldn't you imagine doing without?
- If all jobs paid the same wage and had the same level of recognition, what would you choose to do?
- What gives you energy?
- If you were gifted a bonus day, where money was no object and you could be magically transported to a place or activity of your choosing, where would you go and what would you do?
- If you had three months to spend with a world expert in something – where they would teach you all they know – who would it be and what would they teach you?

Step four – find your element

> 'A musician must make music, an artist must paint, a poet must write, if he has to be ultimately at peace with himself. What a man can be, he must be.'
> **Abraham H. Maslow**

The fourth step is to find what Sir Ken Robinson, a thought leader in the field of human potential, coined the element: where your strengths and passions combine. I highly recommend his book, *The Element,* to learn more.

Finding your element is crucial, because aligning with only your strengths or only your passions in isolation won't lead you to your purpose. Let me use my own career briefly to illustrate. My key strengths (identified by the tool at *stevechamberlain.co.uk/livingonpurpose*) are that I'm a people developer, an emotion feeler and a clarity bringer, and my passions include psychology and all things personal development. My element is where these two areas meet, which for me is coaching and training in the field of human potential. Therefore, when I'm on stage facilitating leadership training, I am in my element. I experience a state of flow, my energy spikes and I find my tribe – others like me – in the fellow coaches and facilitators I work alongside.

Now imagine I'm on the same stage delivering training on a subject for which I hold no passion. While it would still be playing to my strengths, I'd no longer be in my element. It wouldn't matter if I was being paid ten times the amount to deliver the training, or if it was a subject my audience members found fascinating, I still wouldn't experience the same state of flow or enjoyment.

I'd also be out of my element if I was still working in the field of psychology (my passion) but, rather than delivering training, I was instead asked to collate data from research studies (definitely not a strength!). Neither would I find my tribe in either of these places. Therefore, it's only when both our strengths and passions come together that our element comes into play; where we excel and experience true fulfilment.

You will naturally have a range of different strengths and passions, and will therefore be in your element whenever and wherever these come together, both in your professional and personal life. An extraordinary life is one in which you are in your element consistently, and becoming conscious of your strengths and passions makes this possible. The following questions are designed to get you thinking about your element, and what your life and career might look like if you were to live and work within it.

If I knew anything was possible, what would I do?

This question opens your mind up to possibilities you may previously have been too inhibited to explore. Over the course of our lifetime, we get taught to shrink our dreams down from truly aspirational – 'I want to be an astronaut, so I can discover aliens', as my son often tells me excitedly – to 'realistic' – 'I want to reach the next pay grade' – by the time we're adults. But who's to say what's *realistic* for anybody? Every society includes individuals who go way beyond 'realistic' expectations, smashing their Teachers' or parents' perceptions of what was possible for them. Phenomenal sports stars, such as Serena Williams, or great leaders, such as former President Obama, knew to dream big. If these individuals believed they had to aim for what was 'realistic', they could never have achieved their individual feats. They instinctively knew that anything was possible if they stayed in their element and put the hard work in.

What work would feel like play, so I'd never want to retire?
This question puts us in touch with our deepest desires, which may have lain dormant, but never go away. All of us have something we enjoy so much that it feels like we're playing when we do it. Something it would feel painful to be told we couldn't do anymore. You know you're in your element when you're both brilliant and passionate at the same time. This doesn't mean your career won't involve effort, dedication and commitment, as well as challenges along the way, but you'll love the process as well as the outcome. Build your career around your element and you can *play*, rather than *work* for a living.

YOUR JOURNEY

Finding your element

Give yourself a few minutes to consider the following questions and jot down whatever arises for you:
* When and where do you currently feel in your element? List all the activities and roles you play where your strengths and passions come together.

- Look at your list of strengths and consider how you might link each of these with a passion, either in your work or personal life. Do the same for your list of passions, this time considering where you could combine these with any of your strengths.
- Highlight any key strengths or passions that aren't currently being utilised in your life and brainstorm how you might be able to do so going forwards.
- If you knew anything was possible, how could you live and work in your element to find genuine fulfilment?

To give a flavour of how your life can transform when you live in your element, let me briefly share my personal experience.

When work becomes play

Following the period of turbulence in my late twenties that I touched upon earlier, I joined a charity to head up its business development team. It was a role that filled me with fear, as I had no prior experience in this area, so I bought a book on corporate fundraising to get me up to speed as quickly as possible. I had every intention of reading it – I even remember picking the book up on a number of occasions. But no matter how hard I tried, I couldn't bring myself to begin. Not even a line. During the same period, I signed up to training courses designed to up-skill me in my new role. Once again, try as I might, I couldn't get excited by the content, found the days dragged and had nothing to input during the closing Q&A ⏎

sessions. In the office, I found myself paralysed, procrastinating in a way I'd never experienced in my previous roles. I began to ask how I could be so heartless to not be able to motivate myself for such important work within the charity sector. I committed to redoubling my efforts. Yet the more I tried, the greater my resistance and the more useless I felt. It was as if I'd discovered a huge character flaw that had been lying dormant within me.

Today, I can look back on this experience with relief, self-compassion and even amusement. I now know there was nothing wrong with me. I was simply in a job that aligned with none of my core values and for which I had no sense of purpose. There was no compelling reason as to why I was there or what impact I intended to have. If anything, I was standing in the way of someone who would have been in their element in this role.

Fast-forward to today and things couldn't be more different. I now read personal development, leadership and coaching books at a veracious rate. Training events in this field leave me energised (yes, I'm *that guy* who makes the event overrun because I have so many questions!). And these days, I *never* procrastinate. Clients sometimes ask me how I can work from home and not be distracted by television or other temptations, but I don't encounter this problem. Once we're in our element, we stop working for a living and begin *playing* – and who wants to stop playing?

Step five – find your purpose

The fifth and final step is to find your purpose – what you're *really* here to do – which is informed by the insights gained through each of the previous steps. Seeking a purpose statement can feel like a daunting prospect, so let's cut straight to the chase and give you a working version:

My purpose is to align with my values, and live and work within my element, so that I can add unique value to the world.

You could choose to read no further and this would capture the essence of what you're here to do. You're here to be *you*: to understand who you are, what you stand for, what unique strengths and passions you possess, and to bring these together in service of the greater good. Whether this contribution is on a global, community, or family scale is up to you and will be guided by your values.

While this gives you a broad sense of purpose, honing and refining a statement that's personal to you can prove invaluable. The exercises that follow are designed to help you do just that. Don't worry if you find it difficult initially to answer all the questions, or to articulate your purpose. This may simply be a sign that you need to learn more about your values, strengths and passions, or that you need time to reflect. Wherever you are in relation to this, I recommend going through the exercises to see if your purpose becomes clear now. You can always revisit them at a later date.

Before you begin, check to see whether any of the four common objections to purpose feel true for you, because left unchecked, they can prevent you from moving forwards:

1. 'I don't believe everyone has a purpose; others may well do, but I'm pretty sure I don't.'

In my experience, which includes working with countless coaching clients in this field, we *all* have a purpose, and uncovering it can be transformational. The challenge is that this belief alone will stop you from searching, and when you're not looking for something it's highly unlikely you'll find it.

Until now, you're also likely to have been unaware of your values, strengths and passions. Searching for your purpose without these as guidance means you may have been looking in the wrong place.

Of course, it won't be everyone's purpose to change the world on a global scale. We often associate 'purpose' with individuals such as Mother Theresa or Mahatma Gandhi, and therefore a natural assumption is that only a small handful of individuals will have a purpose at any given time. However, 'purpose' in the sense we're talking about doesn't need to be about changing the world; it can simply be about changing *your* world. For example, if your purpose is *To help reduce social isolation by enabling people to feel included and loved*, then this could be fulfilled within your community, by working or volunteering at a care home, or simply by supporting your elderly neighbours or relatives with day-to-day tasks. For someone else, it may be that the same purpose would compel them to focus on international change. Neither of these interpretations is better or worse than the other; it's simply a case of where our values lead us (in the first instance we may value *community*, *love*, *dignity* and *support*; while in the latter we may value *transformation*, *leadership*, *dignity* and *support*).

2. 'I don't believe it will be possible to make a living from aligning with my purpose.'

> *'I had no idea that being your authentic
> self could make me as rich as I've become.
> If I had, I'd have done it a lot earlier.'*
> **Oprah Winfrey**

This myth can be dispelled by looking at the examples we've already drawn upon. We only need to look at Oprah Winfrey, Barack Obama, Serena Williams or any other person at the top of their game to realise that aligning with our purpose can lead to both extrinsic (including financial) and intrinsic success. It's when we're in our element, and aligned with our values and purpose, that we perform at our peak and become indispensable to the organisations we work for, or add unique value to the world through our own endeavours. Wealth in the form of a healthy bank balance can of course be achieved out of alignment with these factors, but we won't also experience the inner wealth of contentment or fulfilment, which are the preserve of those living their lives *on purpose*.

To help bring this to life in a field that doesn't typically offer high financial rewards, imagine that you work as a Teacher and realise your purpose is *To help children discover their inner confidence.* In the early stage of your career, this will guide the pastoral care you give to your classroom, leading you to identify students lacking in confidence and performing below their expected level, and planning interventions to turn this around. In time, the same purpose may compel you to take on more senior leadership roles, becoming a Deputy-Head and then Head Teacher, where you can shape your school's values and ethos around this purpose. Still further down the line, your purpose may lead you to speak at teaching conferences, to pass on your insights on a national level, or to write books for an international audience. All of this is driven by understanding your purpose, with the by-product being an accelerated career path, and the financial and other rewards that come with it.

It's also important to clarify that the purpose we're talking about here doesn't mean we all need to quit our jobs and launch a charity, or make other dramatic changes. Rather, it's about ensuring that our career path aligns with our element and that we can fulfil our purpose through it. It's only when your life or career is clearly out of alignment with your values, element and purpose that you might consider making more significant life changes.

3. 'I'm not sure I really want a purpose, if it means I have to focus on just one thing for the rest of my life.'

It's a common misconception that your purpose will be specific enough to come under a single achievement or role, such as *To write a book on such and such* or *To start my own company accomplishing X and Y.* However, this is a misunderstanding of purpose, for these are concrete achievements that can be fulfilled, begging the question, what happens to your purpose once they're complete? If you've fulfilled your 'purpose' to write a book by the age of 45, where do you go then? From this perspective, it's likely that your motivation and sense of fulfilment will plummet, as you've already accomplished what you had set out to achieve. Similarly, if you believe your purpose is to fulfil just a single role throughout the course of your lifetime, then you're likely to experience this as limiting and restricting, which is the antithesis of purpose.

To help bring this to life, let's return to the teaching example. If we misunderstood our purpose as simply *To be a Teacher*, then we've already fulfilled our purpose the day we step into the classroom. The prospect of a further 40 years of teaching may leave us feeling rather uninspired! However, the purpose we used earlier – *To help children find their inner confidence* – could potentially be fulfilled without ever stepping foot in a classroom. We may decide that our unique set of strengths and passions leads us to create a series of children's books focused on confidence, or to create an app that teaches children about the principles and mindset that underpin it. From this perspective, our purpose can be fulfilled by following numerous different avenues, and such a purpose can never truly be completed. Even once we've retired, this purpose can still guide our actions, leading us to support our grandchildren as they begin to face life's challenges, or volunteer at a local school.

In this way, your purpose is marked by achievements along your route, rather than one single destination. When you reach a landmark or achieve a goal, you simply come back to your purpose once more and plot a new point on your map, before striding out again. Your decisions will be a result of the interaction between your purpose and values (both constants) and the present circumstances of your life (which are always in flux).

4. 'I believe in purpose, but I think it's something that finds us rather than something that we can proactively seek out.'

Given the elevated status we give to those who have lived their lives *on purpose*, such as Nelson Mandela or Martin Luther King, it's easy for us to believe that they were the 'chosen ones' – granted their purpose by an external force. From this assumption, it would be natural for us to live without seeking purpose, either because we're waiting for a divine voice to miraculously tell us our path, or because we don't believe in God. However, what if it's simply holding this belief that prevents us from uncovering our purpose?

What if, instead of coming from an external source, our purpose actually comes from *within*, and it's through knowing ourselves deeply and asking high-quality questions that we find it? No matter whether we view the answers to these questions as coming from God or our inner wisdom, this opens up the possibility that we *all* have a purpose, and already hold the tools we need to find it. Gandhi once stated, 'I have so much to accomplish today that I must meditate for two hours instead of one.' He didn't passively await divine intervention, but consciously sought his purpose, and connected with his inner guidance and wisdom. The result being he found what he was here to do – *To lead people to freedom through non-violent protest.*

It's on us to actively seek, define and live our purpose. No one else can do this for us, and it's our only path to a truly fulfilling life.

Now that we've dispelled the key common objections, let's begin the journey to finding your unique purpose, by first defining your vision:

Define your vision

The key to finding your purpose is to first begin with a compelling vision that goes beyond all sense of limitation. Those who live a truly purposeful life are crystal clear on what they want their world to look like. They hold a vision so powerful that it drives every action within their lifetime. Mahatma Gandhi had a vision for India, Nelson Mandela for Africa, Rosa Parks for America; each had a clear vision of the world they would love to inhabit. While the full realisation of their vision may not have come to bear, it enabled them to keep going in the face of great prejudice and resistance, to help them deliver remarkable change.

While your purpose may draw you to action at a more local level, understanding what change you'd love to see in the world helps you identify the contribution you're here to make. So, while the scale of some of the questions that follow may initially feel a little disconnected from your everyday life, allow yourself to play with possibilities.

Let's find your personal vision now...

Defining your vision

To find your own compelling vision statement, you're looking for two key components, both of which might seem surprising. The first: that your vision is unachievable within your lifetime; and the second: that it cannot be achieved by you alone. If it doesn't meet these two criteria, you're not yet thinking big enough. You need to think about 'vision' in the same way that an international charity does. For example, Save the Children's vision of *A world in which every child attains the right to survival, protection, development and participation* is, sadly, highly unlikely to become reality in the lifetime of the current CEO. Similarly, it would be impossible for them to achieve this vision alone, as countless companies, charities, governments and individuals across the world would need to work in unison. However, holding this vision for *every* child is the fuel that drives everything that Save the Children does.

It's also important that your vision aligns with your values and passions. We might all want to live in a world without famine or conflict, but this won't necessarily form part of our vision unless you have values such as *equality* or *fairness,* and are drawn to work and research in this area. Your vision will naturally be related to what you care deeply about.

Consider the following questions to help you find your personal vision statement:
- What change do I want to see in the world?
- If anything was possible, how would I want the world to be?

- If the world was a perfect outer reflection of my core values, what would it be like?
- How do my strengths and passions inform the kind of world I would love to see?
- If anything was possible, what world would I love my children or grandchildren to inhabit?
- What would my utopia look and feel like?

Give your imagination free rein and think about what's most important to you, based upon your unique value set and passions – you're aiming for truly aspirational at this stage. This is the grand vision that will help you find your purpose in step two. Examples from past clients include:

- A world that encourages growth, healthy living and a focus on positive experiences.
- A supportive world where everyone is accountable and curious.
- A loving and open world where collaboration and understanding drive the progress of humankind.

Reflect upon your values when crafting your vision statement, as your vision will likely be an outer representation of them. For example, in the first example above, the core values being expressed include *growth*, *health*, and *positivity*. You may also find it helpful to envision the answers as coming from your heart or gut, rather than from your mind, which will be predisposed to more logical answers. Your mind will help you to enact and fulfil your purpose, but it's not the source of it. Everyone who has ever achieved anything remarkable has believed in a world and a reality beyond what currently seems possible, so you're in great company by completing this exercise. ⟲

My vision is a world _____

e.g. a world where everyone fulfils their potential and performs a role they love

Or

My vision is a _____ world in which _____

e.g. a harmonious and loving world in which there is peace, equality and justice

Define your purpose

Now you're ready to focus on your purpose: your unique contribution in this lifetime that will help contribute towards making your vision reality. This time, you're looking for a statement that *is* achievable by you within this lifetime. Your purpose won't necessarily bring about your visionary world, but it will be in perfect alignment with it. Without your vision, it's more challenging to define your purpose. Without your purpose, your vision will remain an idealistic fantasy that you do nothing to bring about. It's the interaction between these two that makes the remarkable achievable by otherwise perfectly ordinary men or women in our society.

Your purpose will be found at the intersection between something you feel compelled to give and something that's needed by the world. It will be in perfect alignment with your values and draw upon your key strengths and passions; those that enable you to make the biggest contribution.

A key consideration when finding your purpose statement is that you want it to be broad enough to encompass a lifetime of action (meaning it's as valid when you're 80 years old as it is today), yet specific enough that you know which opportunities to say no to because they don't align. For example, my own purpose statement is *To help people create and lead extraordinary enlightened lives.* This is broad enough to include coaching, writing, speaking and training, plus any other medium through which I may choose to fulfil my purpose in the future. At the same time, it's specific enough to inform me when an opportunity doesn't align. This purpose helped me to understand that it wasn't right for me to move into the lucrative field of executive coaching, as I would be largely serving the interests of big companies rather than the individual. Instead, it drew me into the field of purpose and fulfilment coaching. It inspired me to write this book and helps me know which clients to work with, all the time ensuring that I stay *on purpose*.

Client case study – Sarah

Sarah had experienced a harrowing upbringing. After the death of her mother when she was just 13, she was left unshielded from an abusive father (who on one occasion hit her so hard that he cracked her ribs) and an equally abusive stepmother. Now in her late forties, Sarah was still haunted by her past and experienced intense anxiety and fear in her daily life. Through the steps that we'll come onto later in this journey, she managed to free herself up from the damaging beliefs that were holding her back and began to enjoy life again.

When we came to purpose, Sarah expressed strong doubt that there would be one for her, given that her life until this point had been primarily about survival. However, she was courageous enough to explore, and subsequently identified her vision: *A free world in which all people and animals are empowered to live authentically and to die with dignity.* ⏎

I then asked the purpose question at the end of our coaching session and Sarah went away to reflect. At the start of our next session she looked more animated than I'd ever seen her. She'd found her purpose: *To give a voice to the voiceless.*

Sarah talked excitedly about how deeply this resonated for her. As a child, she'd felt powerless and weak, and ever since had been compelled to support others – people and animals alike – experiencing the same fate. As if to validate the fact she had struck upon her purpose, Sarah had that very day been nominated for her first ever award in her field, for a poem she had written. In hindsight, she realised the content of the poem was all about giving a voice to the voiceless, although she hadn't been conscious of this when she had penned it several months earlier. It had received heartfelt emotional reviews from readers, who said it had struck a chord with them. She knew that, whether on a small scale within her local community, through the medium of writing or beyond, this was her calling. And the suffering she had experienced now served a purpose, enabling her to empathise, connect with and give a voice to those who felt voiceless.

Let's explore your purpose statement now:

Defining your purpose

Consider the following questions to help you find your purpose statement:

- How can I align my values of [insert values], strengths and passions to contribute towards the realisation of my vision of [insert vision]?
- What are my key strengths and passions, and how could I live and work in my element to help create my ideal world?
- What is my gift to share, and who am I here to serve?
- What change do I want to see in the world and how could I operate in my element to help make this possible?
- What does the world want from me and what am I uniquely positioned to contribute?
- What have I always instinctively known I was here to do?

These questions take you from the big-picture aspirational vision, over which you have little control, to your personal contribution within this lifetime – the imprint you can leave on the world that will make it a better place.

Example purpose statements, which follow from the earlier vision statements, are:
- I inspire mental and physical wellbeing in others through activity and lifestyle.
- I support and challenge people to take accountability for their own lives and to be curious about others.
- I help increase collaboration and understanding between people.

The key here is that your purpose statement will be like a fingerprint, unique to you. You're not aiming for a purpose that sounds impressive, but rather that speaks to you personally. There's no judgement here, and whatever you feel drawn to is right for you. Much like your values and vision, your purpose statement is likely to remain constant over time so, at this stage, you don't want to drill down to goals that will fluctuate. Each of the above purpose statements could have any number of specific goals underneath them, which ⮐

can then evolve over time, without any need to change the purpose statement.

Give yourself the gift of time and have a play with finding your purpose statement now. You'll likely want to try a few iterations and don't worry if doesn't come easily; just keep playing until you have something that resonates.

My purpose is_____
e.g. To promote and contribute to an inclusive society and to inspire others to do the same.

Now test your purpose statement, reworking until it fulfils each of the following criteria.

1. Is your purpose statement timeless? Will it be as relevant when you're 80 years old as it is today?
2. Is it broad enough to include a lifetime of action, yet also narrow enough so you'll know what opportunities to say no to?
3. Is it inspiring and motivating? Will a lifetime in pursuit of this be defined by fulfilment and joy?
4. Is it in perfect alignment with your values and vision, and will it place you in your element? As part of this, feel free to revisit and rework your vision statement.
5. Will your purpose help contribute to the realisation of your vision?

If you now have a working purpose statement, congratulations; the next step explains how you can use this to set your goals. If not, don't worry, as this process can take time and reflection. You can visualise what you've done so far as stirring the melting pot: in time, clarity will follow. The following section will help with this process, and the rest of this book will prove just as valuable, even if you need more time to clarify your purpose.

What now?

'The meaning of life is to find your gift.
The purpose of life is to give it away.'
Pablo Picasso

Use your purpose to set your goals

Once you have clarity on both your vision and purpose, you're able to drill down to your specific goals. What concrete actions and achievements will enable you to fulfil your purpose both now and in the future?

Setting purpose-aligned goals

The easiest way to set purpose-aligned goals is to begin with your long-term aspirational goals, and then work backwards from there to inform your medium- and short-term goals. In effect, you're reverse-engineering your life: starting with what your ideal life would look like, and then working back from that point. Let's break this down into a series of steps: ↪

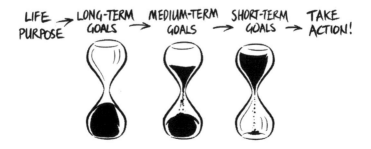

a.   Identifying your long-term goals

The first question to consider is: *'Knowing that my purpose is [add your purpose statement], and that I'm capable of more than I've ever been led to believe, what long-term goals would I love to achieve? What legacy do I want to leave behind?'*

Then see what materialises for you. Each time you write something down, ask yourself *'What else could I do that will help fulfil my purpose?'*

The key here is to come from the assumption that anything is possible. Just because you may not be able to envisage yourself running your own business, winning awards in your field, or speaking on national television right now, it doesn't mean you won't be capable of this ten, twenty or thirty years from now. Your long-term goals here need to leave you feeling both nervous and excited. In the words of Sir Richard Branson, 'If your dreams don't scare you, they are too small.'

b.   Identifying your medium-term goals

Now you're ready to move on to your medium-term goals, likely to be somewhere between five to ten years from now, which will be informed by your long-term goals. The question now becomes:*'Knowing that my purpose is [add your purpose statement], and that my long-term goals are [add long-term goals], what do I plan to achieve [add your target number, for example, five] years from now to ensure I'm both on track and living on purpose?'*

Again, each time you identify a goal, ask yourself *'What else could I do that will help fulfil my purpose?'*

c.   Identifying your short-term goals

Now you're ready to home in on your short-term goals; those you want to focus on from this moment and over the next three to five years. These are the actions and achievements that will build the momentum to make your medium- and long-term goals possible, and by starting with the end in mind, you've ensured that each step you take now is fully aligned with the future you want to create.

'Knowing that my purpose is [add your purpose statement], and that my medium-term goals are [add medium-term goals], what am I compelled to do right now to ensure I'm both on track and living on purpose?'

Once again, ask yourself *'What else could I do that will help fulfil my purpose?'* until you've exhausted all possibilities for now. Remember that, ultimately, there will always be more you can do. Therefore, your purpose statement will serve as a guide throughout your lifetime, taking you to ever-increasing levels of impact. You may find yourself achieving things that, right now, seem like an impossible goal, at which point you can revisit your purpose statement to recalibrate and set even loftier goals.

d. Refine your goals

Now you've completed your list of goals, it's time to do a quick sense check to make sure they're what is often referred to as SMART (Specific, Measurable, Attainable, Relevant and Time-bound). This is a jargon-y way of saying, are they realistic, achievable and motivating goals that will take you in the direction you wish to go? For example, a goal such as *Write an article* is vague and far less motivating than *Write an article of 2,000 words that shares key insights from my research, and send this to five potential journals by the end of June.*

Client case study – Anna

Anna worked for a global corporation, where she'd built a successful career in a role she enjoyed. I've learnt over the years not to expect my client's purpose to tally with their present career path, but I have to admit that Anna's – *To help people lead longer, healthier lives through teaching them nature's capacity to heal* – wasn't something I would have guessed. However, it turned out that, despite being highly valued by her workplace, this wasn't Anna's passion and didn't place her in her element. Ever since she was a child, she'd always been fascinated by health and wellbeing, and it was an area she studied with interest in her spare time.

We used the future visioning exercise to map out her ideal long-term goals and Anna achieved instant clarity; she wanted to be leading her own wellbeing centre, focused on nutrition and natural remedies, where she would also be a practitioner. When we explored this further, the location was Spain and she knew precisely the kind of clients she would be serving, as well as the experience they would receive. We tested this against an alternative future reality, where she continued along her current career path, and she was clear that her current trajectory wasn't right for her, even though it had served her well until this point.

Through medium-term planning, Anna clarified how many clients she would have and what qualifications she would hold ten years from now. We then moved to short-term planning and Anna decided that now was the time to begin training in her chosen field, as well as researching locations for her future venture. However, Anna felt no need to rush this stage, as she still enjoyed her present role, which would ultimately fund this transition. She set a series of short-term goals to begin creating this future reality and got cracking, all without the need to hand in her notice or take on any unnecessary risk until the time was right.

Living on the line

You now know the three most crucial elements of leading a fulfilling and meaningful life: understanding your values (who you are), your vision (the world you wish to inhabit) and your purpose (what you're here to do in service of that vision). If life is a journey, your values represent your compass, and your vision is the North star that guides you. When you live your life on the line between these two you are living *on purpose*, which is where true meaning and fulfilment lie.

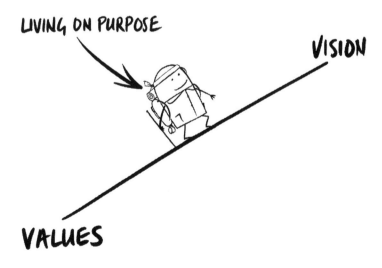

Your values, vision and purpose are unique to you and are therefore the only instruments that can guide your distinct journey. The path that's right for one person will inevitably be wrong for another. The further you stray from your line, the more stress you will experience and the more lost you will feel. Therefore, you're not here to follow someone else's line, but to find your own unique path and stay in alignment.

In a constantly changing world, it will be the unique interplay between your values, vision and purpose *and the circumstances of your life at any given point in time* that will determine right action. What they inform you to do when you're twenty will be markedly different from what you're compelled to do when you're forty or sixty.

You'll notice that your energy peaks when you're living life on your line; you attract opportunities and synchronicities that help you on your way; you make your unique contribution; you often earn more; and you certainly play more. People who live on the line experience true prosperity and abundance, and often don't want to retire. Oprah lives on the line. Obama lives on the line. Gandhi and Einstein lived on the line. It's possible now for each of us to do so.

Setting yourself up for success

Now you have the instruments you need, and your purpose and goals set, it's decision time. Do you put these away in a drawer to gather dust, or do you choose to build your life around them? It's only by taking consistent values- and purpose-aligned actions that your life will transform, so you need to find a way to bring these into your everyday consciousness.

Consider the routines of the great explorers of our past. When on an expedition to uncharted territory, what's the first thing each of them will have done upon rising? Consult their compass and check their bearings before mapping the day's course. They would then continue to check their progress throughout the day, course-correcting where appropriate. This very deliberate routine would be followed until their journey was complete. This is how we guarantee we're travelling in our intended direction; by leaving nothing to chance. And so it is for you on your own unique journey into previously uncharted territory. Your daily Purpose Primer constitutes your compass (values), your North star (vision), your direction of travel (purpose) and your landmarks (goals) all rolled into one.

Building your Purpose Primer

Refer once again to your Purpose Primer (you can download this for free at *stevechamberlain.co.uk/livingonpurpose*) and add your vision, purpose and goals to the values already recorded.

Now decide when, where and how you'll engage with your Purpose Primer. For example, you may decide to read it each working day at 8.30am (the when), on your commuter train (the where), by accessing a document saved on your phone (the how). As a final step, until this habit is formed — broadly considered to be around the twentieth time of repeating a new behaviour — set a reminder to make sure you don't accidentally miss a day. Make a commitment to doing this as part of your daily routine. In the same way that you *always* find the time to brush your teeth, no matter how busy the day ahead, such is the level of commitment required here. Failure to do so in the first instance will lead to tooth decay; failure to do so in the second will lead to the gradual erosion of the life you want to lead.

When:
Where:
How:
Reminder set (Y/N):
How committed am I to doing this?*

Remember, it's only through commitment and action that you turn positive intention into life-changing results.

Re-shaping your life

The above exercises might have led to the realisation that your life is already closely aligned to your values and newly defined purpose, and therefore doesn't require a major overhaul. However, you may still experience states such as low self-confidence or anxiety; find the busyness of life overwhelming; feel you're not performing at the level you aspire to; or still lack true contentment. If this is the case, the remaining stages of this journey are designed to address each of these areas and will help you transform the quality of your life, without necessarily needing to dramatically change the content.

On the other hand, the same exercises may have led to the realisation that your current life trajectory is clearly out of alignment with your values, vision and purpose. Does this mean it's time to quit your job, change your relationships, or overhaul your life in some other way? Possibly, but not necessarily, and even if that's your decision, it's important your transition is well thought through and delivers the best possible outcome for all involved. Knee-jerk decisions, such as handing in your notice without a clear plan of action, can lead to acute stress and are unlikely to be your best course of action.

A valuable first line of enquiry is whether your current job, or area of focus, can be easily realigned around your values and purpose. For example, in your career, if you value *growth* and *impact*, but feel you've been stagnating in your current role, you could ask your manager for new responsibilities that excite and challenge you, or take on a training qualification that will open up new possibilities. Alternatively, you could look internally for other roles that align with your values and purpose, or to external roles that offer a new challenge. The key here is that a change for change's sake is not the answer. It's all about alignment, and if you find a solution already close at hand, that could be the ideal outcome.

If, upon reflection, you decide a major life overhaul is needed, then mapping out the steps to make this reality is the way to go. For example, if you decide your current career doesn't align with your values or purpose, but pays well and supports your family, you could set a two-, five- or even ten-year plan to transition to your new chosen profession. You can then map out the steps you'll need to take in the meantime to prepare for this transition. This could include undertaking additional training, building connections in your new field, downsizing your house or monthly outgoings to build up savings, or whatever else is appropriate.

If handled with forethought, even major life transitions can be undertaken with relative ease. The knock-on effect is that, by choosing to remain in your current job in order to support the transition, your present role actually becomes part of your purpose – a stepping stone on your journey. As a result, you may notice your resistance (and therefore stress) diminishes somewhat. As with anything in life, striking the right balance is key. It's fine to set a ten-year plan if that's genuinely appropriate to your life circumstance and the scale of transition you plan to make. However, if you're putting off what you truly value for the sake of 'security' then this may not serve you. You'll know if you're off-track if you start to feel frustrated or powerless again, at which point you might want to revisit your timeframes and ensure they're taking you where you want to go as quickly as possible.

Carving your own path

You may find that, once you have clarity on your values, vison and purpose, no career in the current job market truly aligns. If that's the case, you may feel compelled to create something new. This is the space entrepreneurs inhabit and may be where you're drawn. If so, the good news is it's now easier to set up your own business and reach your target market than at any previous time in history. Before the digital age, you would have needed significant capital to establish a company in order to cover the costs of property, staffing, printing, distribution and so on. Since the advent of the internet, and the subsequent developments in global ecommerce and distribution, a highly lucrative business that adds significant value to the world can be set up with relatively little capital. Just look at the teenagers with a talent for vlogging who are running successful businesses from their bedrooms, or the home-run ecommerce businesses with customers around the world. As with transitioning your job, if this is your chosen path, you'll want to map out the steps carefully, to ensure you don't expose yourself to unnecessary risk. However, if you add genuine value to the world, the rewards – both financial and intrinsic – can be immense.

Clarifying your ideal career path or business

If you feel your purpose compels you to set a new career path in motion or start your own business, but you're unsure of what that might like look, this exercise is designed to help give you clarity.

Step one – use your values and purpose to brainstorm possible career paths or business opportunities
Consider the following questions and jot down any thoughts that occur. Resist the temptation to evaluate options as they arise – at this stage, every idea is worth capturing. Simply keep coming back to the same question until all your ideas are exhausted:

- Which potential career paths/business opportunities align with my values of [insert values], and my purpose to [insert purpose]?
- What could I do that would allow me to operate in my element and live my values of [insert values]?
- If I knew that my earnings would increase the more I enjoyed my work, what would I choose to do?
- What business or career path does my purpose compel me to build?

Don't move on to stage two until you're confident you've exhausted all possible paths, so keep asking 'What else?' until you have a comprehensive list.

Step two – decide on the criteria your career path or business must fulfil

You'll need some criteria by which to decide whether a potential career path or business is right for you. The below questions will offer clarity:

- Are you looking to run your own business, or does your purpose draw you to work for a company or charity?
- What level of income are you aiming for?
- Are you looking to work alone or with others?
- Where do you want to be based (for example, working from home/in an office)?
- Do you want to travel and, if so, how much? Nationally or internationally?
- What key strengths do you want to be utilising?
- What passions do you want your career or business to align with?
- How many days do you want to work?
- In order to fully align with your values of [insert core values] and purpose to [insert purpose], what other criteria are crucial to this decision?

Step three – check your brainstormed ideas against your criteria

Take each of your brainstormed ideas from stage one and check whether they meet your newly defined criteria. While it's unlikely any will meet all your criteria perfectly, use this process to identify your top three possibilities.

Step four – check in with your gut instinct

Evaluate your top three possibilities by answering the questions below. Your mind won't know which is the right or wrong path, but *you* will, so tune into your heart or gut:

- Which of these paths most closely aligns with my values of [insert core values] and purpose to [insert purpose]?
- Which path would make me happiest? ↵

- Which path would I find most fulfilling?
- Which path would see me adding most value to the world?
- Which path would I not want to retire from?
- Which path would allow me to leave a compelling legacy?
- Projecting forwards five, ten and twenty years from now, what plays out for me on each of these paths?

Getting more data

As we touched upon earlier, it's possible you don't yet have enough data to go on to clarify your purpose; you may have untapped strengths lying dormant, or passions you're yet to discover. If this is the case, try new things, take on new roles, explore, test and play. When informed by your values and guided by your energy, this process will be rewarding in and of itself, and can be viewed as part of your journey to purpose; just as vital as anything you'll do further down the line.

The clues to discovering your purpose lie in many places, and can be so subtle as to be overlooked, so it's important you stay alert. In my own life, as a child, I often got flashes of a future me working 1:1 with people to help them overcome their problems. I had an innate capacity for understanding who was suffering and felt an inner desire to help them, even though I was too young to do anything about it. Later in life, even in job roles I didn't enjoy, there were further clues, such as the fact I always relished training other people and passing on knowledge when the opportunity arose. I was also the one who helped others to summon up the courage to make their next career move. Looking back, I already knew what I was here to do. It just took me a while to actually listen! What have you always known you're here to do?

It's also possible that life may have a different plan for you than the one you currently envisage. For example, we hear of people who lose a loved one to a rare disease who then feel compelled to set up a charity or support group to change the world for the better. In such instances, you could say that your purpose finds *you*, rather than you seeking *it*. If a significant life event seems to draw you to a different path – which we could call fate – then view this as valuable new data. You can revisit the steps outlined here at any point in your journey, determine whether your values, vision or purpose have changed, draw a new line and navigate accordingly. Nothing you'll have done until that point will have been lost, but your onward journey will lead you to different terrain and new opportunities.

It's also important you stay open to any data that suggests you've strayed off-track. This will typically come in the form of a dip in motivation, restlessness, or a broader sense of feeling unfulfilled. If this happens, revisit the values and purpose exercises, to explore whether anything has changed, redraw your line and set out once more.

Trust in life

A life lived *on purpose* is a delicate balance between conscious choice and surrender. Having a clear plan of where you want to go is invaluable, but if you stick to this too rigidly, you may miss unexpected opportunities along the way. When you're *on purpose,* life will ultimately guide your journey, opening up opportunities and chance meetings that you could never have predicted or controlled. Your purpose and life are intimately entwined: your role is to stay open to whatever comes your way, and to grasp opportunities that align with your purpose.

Your role, then, in a purpose-driven life, is to be a co-creator, where you consciously steer your life, while also remaining open to signs and chance connections that life is giving you. Just like all explorers, you map out where you intend to go, and then respond in the moment as the unexpected appears over the horizon.

Synchronicity at play

Within a few weeks of aligning my life around my newly discovered purpose, I had more chance meetings and synchronicities than I'd ever encountered in the previous ⮌

decade. Within just two weeks of deciding to set up my own coaching practice, I had a chance introduction to one of the UK's leading coaches — Elke Edwards — who had just sold her executive development business to set up a purpose-driven enterprise — Ivy House[7] — and was on the lookout for purpose-driven coaches. I am now one of Ivy House's performance coaches, bringing life-changing learning to the UK's next generation of leaders, both in businesses and schools, which is in perfect alignment with my purpose. I couldn't have engineered this if I'd tried, as I had never come across Elke or Ivy House before, but life drew us together.

---

7 If you would like to find out more about Ivy House's work, please visit *ivyhouse.co.uk*

Purposeful retirement

Building a purpose-driven life is just as achievable and important if you're retired. Retirement simply means you no longer fulfil a paid role. But moving on from your career frees up a significant amount of time and space through which your next contribution can be made. It's as important to have a vision of the world you wish to inhabit and pass on to the next generation at retirement age as it is in your youth. You also benefit from the knowledge and wisdom that comes with time, something that's so undervalued by modern western societies. Given that you now have more space in which to play and create, what contribution do you choose to make to the world?

Of course, how and where you make your contribution will be influenced by your present health and life circumstances. But we only need to look at the lifetime contribution of individuals such as Stephen Hawking to realise that even the most severe of life's challenges, such as motor neurone disease, needn't hold us back from having a profound impact on our world. The following exercise is designed to get you thinking about how retirement can be equally as fulfilling as any other stage of your journey.

Setting your purpose for retirement

Whether you're currently retired, or are approaching retirement age, the following questions will help you clarify your purpose at this stage:

- Knowing my values are [insert core values], my vision is [insert vision], and my purpose is [insert purpose], what am I here to achieve in this moment?
- What have I learned on my journey that I wish to pass on to the next generation?
- What impact do I want to have in relation to my family, my community, my country, or my world?
- What legacy do I choose to leave?

Wherever you are on your life journey, and whether you now have a purpose statement or are on the path towards doing so, the remaining stages of this book will prove just as relevant. You can revisit the above exercises at any time you feel in need of further clarity.

Bringing it all together

The fascinating thing about discovering your purpose is that it's been there all along, within you, just like your values. You simply had to ask the right questions to uncover it. And knowledge is power. From the moment you know what you're here to accomplish, you're able to drive your life like never before.

A purposeful life is, by definition, a life of contribution. You are quite literally adding *value* to the world by honouring your values and aligning with your purpose. And, by fulfilling your purpose, you achieve fulfilment for yourself. By asking each day where you can add value, you play your own unique part in changing our world for the better.

A purposeful life is not the reserve of a select few individuals, but is the calling for each of us. Imagine what our society would look and feel like if every member lived a life fully aligned with their values and purpose. It's within your power to step up and make this your reality. When you go to play rather than to work, to contribute rather than to take, you'll know you're truly living *on purpose* and, in so doing, will light the way for others to follow.

However, knowing your purpose is one thing. Having the belief system, mindset and skillset to make this your reality is another. The rest of this journey is about giving you the insights and tools that will enable you to live *on purpose*.

Reflection

- What are you *really* here to do?
- What legacy do you wish to leave?
- What is your key insight from this stage of your journey, and what will you do differently as a result?

STAGE THREE
CARVING YOUR BELIEF SYSTEM

Beliefs – what do you believe and does it serve you?

'Until you make the unconscious conscious,
it will direct your life and you will call it fate.'
Carl Jung

'Whether you think you can or you
think you can't, you're right.'
Henry Ford

Your belief system holds the key to living *on purpose*. If you don't truly believe you're capable of reaching your destination, then that will be the reality you create. Every great explorer from our past had a belief system that enabled them to move beyond old perceived limitations and step into the unknown, overcoming obstacles and staying the course when the going got tough. It's therefore crucial that you consciously select beliefs that take you where you want to go.

Your actions and the resulting circumstances of your life serve as a mirror for your underlying belief system. We often spend our lives on the surface, trying to change the conditions of our situation – our job, our relationships, our possessions – rather than looking at what's going on a little deeper. This is the equivalent of deciding to buy a new mirror when we don't like what we see in our reflection. Ultimately, nothing has changed and the dissatisfaction returns. It's only by reshaping your belief system that you achieve real, lasting change in your life, freeing you up to stay *on purpose*.

What are beliefs?

> '*Don't believe everything you think.*'
> **Wayne Dyer**

Beliefs are simply thoughts that you buy into; nothing more and nothing less. Until you believe a thought to be true, it remains just that – a thought – but once you've consciously or subconsciously accepted it, it becomes a belief and begins to influence your behaviour. For example, when considering adopting a vegan diet, on the one hand you may have thoughts such as, 'It seems natural for humans to eat animals because our ancestors did,' or conversely, 'After watching that programme about global warming, it doesn't seem to be sustainable for humans to continue to eat meat.' At this point, these are simply thoughts – you haven't yet come down on one side of the equation. But if we jump forwards to a point where you've explored your options and taken a decision, you'll have started to form more solidified beliefs, such as, 'Eating meat is perfectly normal,' or conversely, 'Eating animals is unsustainable.' The choices you make will start to look very different and, in time, you may find yourself drawn into disagreements with people who hold a different belief to you.

The point here is not whether choosing to eat meat is good or bad; it's that beliefs drive our behaviour, and our rigid or fixed beliefs begin initially as fluid thoughts. In this way, beliefs are formed through a similar process to water (thoughts) turning into ice (beliefs) under certain conditions. Much like ice, your beliefs shape your world once solidified. In the same way that icebergs might prevent a ship from following its chosen path, your rigid beliefs may prevent you from taking certain courses of action. And, just as your view may be blocked by an iceberg, so too your fixed beliefs prevent your mind from seeing the world as it is without bias. As such, your beliefs shape the way you see the world and act as a filter for the information you take in.

Surprisingly, many of our beliefs are unlikely to have been consciously chosen. There was never a day at school when your Teacher laid out a range of possible beliefs for you to examine, test and then select. Instead, through a process akin to osmosis, many of your beliefs will have been passed on imperceptibly to you, via your early experiences, and the wider social and cultural contexts in which you've grown up.

Even though you never chose them, your beliefs have driven your behaviour and created your present life. The world you experience is the result of your perception, and your perception is the result of your beliefs about *yourself* and *your world*.

Beliefs about the world

Do you experience the world as it truly is, or do your inherited beliefs taint what you see?

Imagine you have been brought up in a household defined by fear. Your parents share fundamental beliefs that *People can't be trusted* and *The world isn't a safe place,* and see it as their role to teach you about the dangers that exist to keep you safe. They repeatedly warn you about the risk of being by yourself or trusting strangers, and your life until this point has been a sheltered one. As a young child, your parents' view of the world is all that you know and trust, so hearing them verbalise these beliefs will naturally shape your own. What influence might these adopted beliefs have on your perception of the world?

THEIR JOURNEY

Client case study – Julie

Julie had suffered from an extended period of sexual abuse as a child. When we began working together, she was in her forties and her entire adult life until that point had been defined by fear, mistrust and anxiety. In our first session, it took twenty minutes for her to summon the courage to step into my coaching studio, as she believed small spaces were dangerous and that men were a threat. I spoke very little in that first session together, other than to draw Julie's attention to everything that was safe in the environment – the clean air she could breathe; the comfortable chair she was sitting on; the view of the trees out of the window – to begin the process of questioning the validity of her old beliefs. In our second session, it took just five minutes for her to enter the space, and by our third session (by which time we'd examined and reworked some of her old untrue and unhelpful beliefs), she was able to walk straight in, reporting low anxiety.

Julie's beliefs about the world, while completely under-standable given her challenging past, were now preventing her from leading the life she wanted. She had a very limited circle of friends, none of whom were men, and was constantly on high alert. When she went out for dinner with her family, she would deliberately pick a table where she could sit with her back to the wall, with a clear line of sight to the door. She was then able to scan and assess everyone who entered the restaurant, checking for potential sources of danger. In reality, of course, there was no danger, but her previously unchallenged beliefs created and reinforced this highly stressed state.

In our sessions, we evaluated the validity of beliefs such as, 'The world is a dangerous place' and 'Men are untrustworthy' and, when Julie realised these thoughts weren't one hundred per cent true (for not *everywhere* in the world is dangerous and not *every* man a liar) or helpful (they created chronic anxiety in her life), she reworked them to form new beliefs, such as 'Men and women are all equal and are at different stages on their own journey. I choose to spend my time with people I resonate with.'

Following this work, Julie excitedly came into a subsequent session, telling me about a breakthrough moment at a family occasion, where she'd sat happily at a table in the middle of the restaurant and had felt no compulsion to scan the room. Instead, for the first time she could remember, she'd given her full attention to her family members. She also now felt more comfortable with men and had experienced her first uninterrupted night's sleep that she could remember in her adult life. Julie is now thriving, setting up the next exciting stage of her life.

Beliefs about ourselves

This effect plays out just as powerfully with beliefs we hold about ourselves. Imagine you're standing backstage five minutes before being introduced to deliver a thirty-minute presentation to a group of one hundred work colleagues and clients. It's on a subject you know well and you have learned the content by heart, but you have your speech notes in your pocket just in case. How might your beliefs impact upon your experience here?

Let's first imagine you hold two deeply held beliefs: 'I'm useless at public speaking,' and 'It's not OK to make mistakes.' The natural result of these beliefs is a fight or flight response. No matter the number of hours you've put into prepping, you've told yourself you're incapable of the challenge at hand and that anything other than a perfect presentation isn't acceptable, so you'll naturally want to escape. Your breathing becomes shallow, your mouth feels dry and worst-case scenarios begin to flash through your mind. Adrenaline courses through your body, inhibiting the recall capacities of your brain, which are precisely what you need in order to remember and deliver your presentation.

As you're introduced on stage, your mind goes blank and you find yourself pulling the notes out of your pocket, standing stock still behind the 'shield' of the lectern. You deliver a nerve-wracking, stumbling presentation, barely looking up from your notes. As you step off the stage thirty minutes later, you've reaffirmed your belief that you're terrible at public speaking and, even worse, tell yourself you're a failure. You do everything you can to avoid stepping on stage again in the future, because of these deep-rooted beliefs.

Now let's rewind this particular scenario: you're backstage again, five minutes before the presentation. You've done the same preparation, know your content by heart and again have the notes in your pocket. This time, however, you hold different beliefs: 'I'm well prepared,' and 'Some nerves are natural, but I can handle this.' What plays out now? The fight or flight response is no longer activated. You may still feel nervous, but you perceive this as normal and are able to reframe this as excitement about stretching beyond your comfort zone. As a result, your system isn't flooded with adrenaline and your breathing remains normal.

Your name is called and you step on stage. This time, despite your natural nerves, you recall your presentation easily from memory and feel comfortable stepping aside from the lectern, making eye contact with your audience as you begin. After a minute or so of talking, you begin to feel at ease and, although at one point you stumble over your words, you're able to laugh it off, take a deep breath and regain your flow. By the end of the presentation, you feel energised and you leave the stage with your notes still firmly in your pocket. You feel safe to evaluate your performance and, as a result of positive feedback, now believe you're quite good at presenting, although you're intent on improving further and put yourself forward for future speaking opportunities, to help accelerate this journey.

The only thing that changed in this scenario was the beliefs. The difference in outcome and experience, however, was huge.

Our beliefs shape our world and drive our behaviour in a profound way, yet we're typically unconscious of them. Crucially, many of our beliefs aren't even accurate and don't serve us. As such, your beliefs can become like a mental prison, where your mind only attends to information that confirms your view of the world and ignores or disregards that which doesn't. Each belief that isn't true, or that doesn't serve you, is a bar in your prison cell. *I am lazy*, internalised after a Teacher criticised you at school, leads to procrastination and lack of effort as an adult, which we then see as confirming the validity of the belief. *Life is a competition,* internalised after messages from your parents, becomes the 'truth' for you and leads to a life defined by stress, which again confirms our view of a competitive world.

We view the world through our own filter. One person who believes the world is a safe and friendly place will inhabit a different world to another who believes the world is dangerous and threatening. They may both live in the same city, but they'll choose different friends, jobs and lifestyles based on their view of the world, and will experience different thoughts and emotions. They'll also elicit different reactions from people they meet and will build different relationships. In this way, your beliefs are both a creative and self-fulfilling force; they create the outer circumstances that reflect their perceived truth.

My glass ceiling

I'll always remember the moment my boss, founder of The London Business Forum where I worked, told me that, from that moment on, it would be my responsibility to introduce speakers at our events on stage and facilitate the Q&A sessions that followed. My heart lurched, adrenaline started pulsing through my body and visions of freezing on stage flashed through my mind. I'd just discovered my glass ceiling: the imaginary limit that my beliefs told me I couldn't move beyond.

Until that moment, I'd loved my role on event days: looking after front-of-house operations, welcoming delegates and helping to create a positive event atmosphere. However, getting up on stage to introduce figures such as Bob Geldof, Tom Peters and Lord Sebastian Coe in front of 500 people wasn't possible for 'someone like me'. ↩

While I knew I had limiting beliefs, at this point in my life I didn't know I had the ability to test their validity or reshape them. Therefore, what followed was a period of intense anxiety in the build-up to event days. On the day itself, I'd often disappear into the bathroom to practice my lines in an attempt to get them *word perfect* – something I now know to be a source of unnecessary pressure – and would wait nervously backstage to introduce the speaker. At one event, my worst fears were realised: I forgot my lines and froze. At another, I was so nervous before going out, I thought I was going to have a panic attack – something that did happen a few days later during a lunchbreak. These experiences led to me quitting my job, because I believed I couldn't cope with the pressure – a belief that led to much darker times ahead.

I'm delighted to say none of the above now plays out for me, because I understand the power of beliefs and the process of reshaping them. I have consciously chosen beliefs that are true and helpful. I now facilitate sessions with some of the most talented emerging leaders in the country with Ivy House and love public speaking. Because of my experiences, I'm now able to help others break through their own glass ceilings and, without exception, find that a combination of true and helpful beliefs enables people to thrive, whatever the situation at hand.

While beliefs can impact heavily upon your life, by understanding they're simply thoughts that you've bought into, you come to realise that *you* have the power to change them.

Becoming aware of your beliefs

Before deciding whether your beliefs serve you or not, you first need to bring them into your conscious awareness. You don't need to look at all your beliefs, just the big players. What are your core beliefs that shape your views of yourself and your world, and therefore have a direct impact on your experience of it?

Finding your core beliefs

Step one: identify your beliefs about the world

The below sentence starters are designed to help you identify your beliefs about the world (anything outside of you). Set aside a few minutes and write down as many completions to each sentence as you can, before moving on to the next. It's important to go with your first, instinctive answer, rather than spending time considering it. You're looking for any beliefs that you instinctively feel might be holding you back in some way (for example, 'Life is hard').

- Life is...
- People are...
- Money is...
- Relationships are...
- Work is...
- The world is...

Next, think of any areas in your life where you consistently struggle. Ask what additional beliefs you currently hold about these situations that might be having an impact. For example, if your job involves sales, but you find meeting your targets a challenge, do you hold a belief such as 'Making sales is hard' or 'The targets we're set are impossible to achieve'? Or, if you find yourself regularly in conflict with friends ↩

or family members, do you hold the belief that 'Friendships are complicated,' or 'Conflict is unavoidable'?

Finally, think of someone with whom you regularly experience conflict, such as a boss, family member or friend. Bring to mind a recent example where their behaviour disturbed you, and ask which rigid beliefs you hold that might have contributed to this conflict (for example, 'My manager should *always* show their appreciation for the overtime I put in').

- They should...
- They shouldn't...
- They need to...
- They have to...

Step two: identify your beliefs about yourself

In this step, there's initially just one sentence for you to complete – *I am...* – which gets straight to the core of your beliefs about yourself. Again, set aside a few minutes and write down as many completions to this sentence as you can. Once more, you're looking here for any beliefs that you instinctively feel might be holding you back in some way (for example, 'I am a failure,' 'I am shy,' or 'I am boring'). What do you secretly fear might be true, that you don't want anyone to know?

- I am...
- I am...
- I am...
- I am...
- I am...

Now consider any situations in your life where you consistently struggle to achieve either the outcomes you desire or the inner state you would love to experience, and complete the sentences below. For example, if you always feel stressed before meetings, do you believe, 'I shouldn't find this so difficult,' or 'I need to be perfect'?

- I should...
- I shouldn't...
- I need to...
- I have to...

Next, ask which additional beliefs you currently hold about yourself that might play a part during these scenarios. For example, if you find yourself shouting at your kids more often than you'd like, do you believe, 'I am highly strung,' or even, 'I am a bad parent'? If you're often late delivering work projects, do you believe, 'I am a procrastinator,' or 'I am a perfectionist'? If anything comes up for you, add these below.

- I am...
- I am...
- I am...
- I am...
- I am...

Finally, scan this list of commonly held limiting beliefs and circle any that resonate:

- I am a bad person
- I am unlucky
- I am a pessimist
- I am weak
- I am unworthy
- I am unlovable
- I am a victim
- I am vulnerable
- I am stupid ⏎

- I am a fraud
- I am boring
- I am a worrier
- I am a stressed person
- I am an anxious person
- I am a depressed person
- I am insincere
- I am a procrastinator

Step three: identify beliefs that will move you off purpose

The final stage is to ask which additional beliefs you hold, either in relation to yourself or your world, that will stop you from living on your line and fulfilling your purpose. For example, if your purpose involves motivating people to take action, but you don't believe you're capable of inspiring others, then this belief alone will hold you back from living *on purpose*. Therefore, ask yourself:

'Knowing that my purpose is [insert purpose], what do I currently believe about myself or my world that will prevent me from stepping up and having maximum impact?'

Record these additional beliefs here.

You now have a snapshot of the beliefs that shape your perception and influence your behaviour every day. These beliefs are like the lenses in a pair of glasses through which you view the world, and each of us has our own unique prescription.

Beliefs that serve you

*'Whatever the mind of man can conceive
and believe, it can achieve.'*
Napoleon Hill

Because your beliefs directly influence your experiences, it's vital they're an accurate reflection of reality, and that they serve you. Until now, the question 'Does this belief serve me?' may have been a difficult one to answer. Serve you in what sense, or in relation to which outcome? However, now you know your values and purpose, you know who you are and where you want to head, meaning the answer can come into sharp focus. Let's look at each of your beliefs and see if they take you where you wish to go.

Do your beliefs serve you?

Begin by selecting one of the beliefs you identified in the last exercise – go for one that you instinctively feel is holding you back at this point in your journey. Returning to our earlier analogy, view this belief as a block of ice, positioned in front of you, ready to be examined. When you're ready, ask the following two simple questions:

- *Is this belief one hundred per cent true? Y/N.* Before answering, understand that to qualify as one hundred per cent true, it would need to stand up in *every* circumstance, and be so watertight as to be passed in a court of law. Therefore, the belief *Money is scarce* would need to be true in *every* situation *always*. There could never be a time when money hadn't been scarce for you, and it would also need to be scarce for everyone else.
- *Is this belief helpful? Y/N.* You'll be able to answer *yes* if this belief helps you achieve both your desired outcome and the emotional state you wish to feel. For example, ↵

the belief *I must win at all costs* may lead to success in the form of accolades, but if it also triggers a state of anxiety rather than inner focus, this belief may no longer be deemed helpful. As part of this, consider whether holding this belief will support you in achieving your purpose; if not, then it can't truly be considered helpful.[8]

Repeat this process for each of your beliefs. If you deem any to be both one hundred per cent true and helpful, you'd be wise to continue to hold it in its current form. If any beliefs don't stand up well to this scrutiny – and don't be surprised if this is the case for most, if not all, of your limiting beliefs! – continue to the next step.

---

8 These questions come from the work of Albert Ellis, the founder of Rational Emotive Behaviour Therapy, and were taught to me by Professor Windy Dryden and Nicola Martin.

How to change beliefs that don't serve you

Many of us might feel wary of examining or reworking our beliefs, for fear we may change something fundamental about who we are. This is why some people are reticent to work with a coach or therapist, even if their life is currently defined by struggle. However, this fear is simply the result of a misconception: that we *are* our beliefs. As we've seen, our beliefs are simply thoughts we buy into, and can change over time, so they cannot be who we are. Therefore, no harm can result from examining or consciously challenging our beliefs, as long as our intention is to make them both true and helpful. From this realisation, we're freed up to explore, examine and adapt our belief system to ensure it truly serves us.

Client case study – Aisha

Aisha was born and raised in Nigeria. In her twenties, she and her husband had moved to England to set up a new life. Now in her late thirties, her children were both at school, and she and her husband were both in full-time employment. However, their children, while bright, were struggling at school and her son, then aged nine, had recently been in tears, desperately resisting doing his homework. Aisha wanted to know how she could change the situation, but felt helpless.

When we explored the incident, it became apparent that Aisha held some rigid beliefs that she'd internalised from her own childhood, such as 'Children *must* succeed at school' and 'It's my job as a parent to make sure they get good grades.' On the surface, these beliefs were well intentioned, but when we investigated further, Aisha realised they were driving behaviour that exacerbated the situation. These beliefs led her to put significant pressure on her children to do their homework and she wouldn't let them play until everything was completed perfectly. She realised she'd taken the fun out of learning and had been unconsciously teaching her children that her love was conditional based on their performance. This naturally led to her children avoiding the stress and fear of doing homework, which in turn triggered a reaction from Aisha.

Aisha tested this belief and realised it wasn't one hundred per cent true, as there was nothing to say they *must* succeed. She might really *want* them to, but not every child must ↵

attain straight A grades. We talked about individuals such as Sir Richard Branson, who'd gone on to achieve incredible success despite struggling at school, and also whether it was realistic to expect children to excel in every subject. Having realised this belief wasn't true, Aisha also understood it wasn't helpful, as it was creating stress and conflict, and was actually pushing her children away from study. She therefore reworked the belief to, 'I want my children to enjoy the process of learning and growing, so they can be the best they can be, and I choose to do everything I can to create an environment that makes this possible.'

Following our work, Aisha let me know the pressure she'd put on herself and her children had dropped away, and she was able to make homework fun and engaging again. Her children are now thriving, and she's since gone on to become a Primary School Teacher, applying many of these lessons in her own classroom.

We used the analogy earlier of thoughts being like water and beliefs like ice. Under the right conditions (the application of heat), ice can return to its liquid form, with the potential to then be reconfigured into a different ice structure under the right conditions (the application of cold). This holds true for our beliefs. Even though a belief may have taken on a sense of permanence for you, you can at any time return it to its more fluid form of thought, with the application of your conscious attention. You can then reconfigure this thought into a more helpful belief through conscious choice. *Every* belief, no matter how seemingly permanent, can be reworked via this process.

Old, untrue and unhelpful beliefs tend to be able to be summed up in very short sentences. Once reworked, these sentences often become much longer, to ensure they are not open to misinterpretation, much like legal documents. The idea is then to capture the essence of this new belief, so that it can be easily remembered and used. Included below are some examples of beliefs my coaching clients have reworked, to give a flavour of what you're aiming for.

Beliefs about the world

Old (untrue and unhelpful) belief: People are cold.

New (true and helpful) belief: Until now, largely because of this untrue and unhelpful belief, I've paid attention to – and spent most of my time with – people who are emotionally cold. However, the world is full of different types of people and it's up to me who I choose to spend my time with. I make a commitment to being warm and friendly myself, and to surrounding myself with people who bring positive energy.

Essence belief: I choose to be warm and loving, and to spend my time with like-minded people.

Old: Work is stressful.

New: In my current job, I've experienced periods of significant stress. However, I've had previous roles where I wasn't stressed at all, and have also experienced days in my current job where I felt calm and confident. Work can be challenging, but ultimately I'm in control of how I handle my workload, and will ask for support as and when I need it.

Essence: Work is what I make of it, and I trust that I can handle anything that arises.

Old: Relationships are difficult and painful.

New: Relationships can be complex, and I've had some painful experiences in the past. However, I've also had some of my peak experiences while in loving relationships and understand that they hold the potential to be deeply rewarding. I choose to learn how to build great relationships, and will be patient and accepting through this process.

Essence: I am committed to building meaningful relationships and choose to be forgiving of myself in the process.

Beliefs about the self

Old: I am stupid.

New: While there have been occasions where I haven't done as well as I'd have liked, I also have lots of achievements and successes that show I'm competent in many ways. Just like everyone else, I have strengths and weaknesses, and I'm committed to developing as much as I can in areas that are important to me.

Essence: I am good enough just as I am, and commit to learning more every day.

Old: I am unlovable.

New: Throughout my life there are lots of examples of people who have expressed love for me. Because of some of my early childhood experiences, I've sometimes struggled to accept and reciprocate this love, but that's understandable and something I'm actively working on. I choose to forgive myself through this process.

Essence: I am learning to love and be loved.

Old: I am weak.

New: Partly as a result of being bullied and my slender physique as a child, I've told myself that I'm weak, which has played out negatively in many areas of my life. However, strength comes in many forms and

I've shown huge character in several areas of my life up to this point. I choose to build a strong, positive mindset and healthy body from this point forwards.

Essence: I choose to step into my innate strength in all areas of my life.

Reworking your beliefs

Take the first of the beliefs you determined as untrue and/or unhelpful, and imagine you've laid it in front of you. Just as you might transform a block of ice into a sculpture, you're now going to deliberately carve out beliefs that truly serve you, by answering the three questions below:

- **How can I rework this belief so that it's one hundred per cent true and would stand up in a court of law?** Using our earlier limiting belief about money, we're not aiming to come up with an affirmation that doesn't ring true here, such as *Money is everywhere*. Just as *Money is scarce* turns out not to be one hundred per cent true when we shine a spotlight onto it, this new thought also isn't accurate. If money was literally everywhere, everyone in the world would be unimaginably wealthy, which we know not to be the case. So, put your lawyer's hat on and craft a statement that's one hundred per cent accurate, such as *Some people have lots of money and some people less.* It's not going to win any literary prizes, but we're not going for flamboyance at this stage – just the truth, the whole truth and nothing but the truth. ⮐

- **How can I rework this belief so it's helpful?** Take the statement you've just carved and make extra refinements, to ensure it serves you as powerfully as possible. For example, *Some people have lots of money and some people less. While I appreciate money doesn't equal happiness, wherever possible I will work to ensure I am prosperous.* This brings in an element of being helpful, in that it offers an intent – to be prosperous – but without unrealistic expectations or a heavy burden (for example, *I will always be wealthy and money will make me happy*). The key here is to avoid including anything you're not one hundred per cent in control of. For example, you're not one hundred per cent in control of your wealth at any given time, as your job may unexpectedly be made redundant, but you can be one hundred per cent in control of your intention – *wherever possible* – to work towards prosperity.

- **How can I capture the essence of this new belief?** Now, aim to capture the essence of this belief to make it succinct and memorable. Where possible, try to refine it down to a single sentence, such as *I choose to give my best, and trust that prosperity will follow.*

Study this newly formed belief as you would an ice sculpture in front of you. Does it make you feel empowered and free? Will it take you where you wish to go? If the answer is *no*, return to the steps above and rework until you're happy. Once the answer is *yes*, write this new belief into your Purpose Primer (download your Purpose Primer for free at *stevechamberlain. co.uk/livingonpurpose*), ready for you to engage with as part of your daily routine. Repeat this process for each of your beliefs.

At this point, you can visualise your new beliefs as fragile, carved precisely as you want them, but not yet permanently frozen. They will only enter this permanent state once they are fully internalised; once you start to live and breathe them, which you do by engaging with them regularly. That said, there's a common misconception that there needs to be considerable time and effort involved in reshaping long-held beliefs. To help dispel this myth, imagine you're living at a time when you, and everyone else on the planet, believe the world to be flat. Imagine also that someone has just invented the first space rocket and you have the opportunity to join them as one of the first astronauts in space. Upon orbiting the Earth and seeing it unquestionably as a sphere, how long would it take you to change your lifelong belief that it's flat? No time. How many daily affirmations would you have to repeat to overwrite this old programming? None. You would, quite literally, see the world differently in an instant.

Now imagine you're led into a pitch-black room and asked to describe what it looks like. Unsurprisingly, you can't. Now imagine someone turns the lights on for five seconds, so you can see everything. After this time has passed, the lights are turned off again and you're asked to describe the room once more. This time, despite being back in darkness, you can do a much better job. This is because you cannot unknow something you now know: your perception has been permanently changed.

The same holds true for your beliefs. Once you've brought them into the light of day, examined them and realised they don't serve you, you can't relate to them in the same way again. This is part of the process of enlightenment. You may experience the same thought or belief out of habit, but you'll now see it in a whole new light. You'll also have your reworked true and helpful belief to hand.

Through this process, you're helping new neural pathways to form in your brain. Rather than trying to override old limiting beliefs through constant repetition, you have cleared the old pathways first, before laying new ones in their place. Some repetition will then, of course, be helpful to enable these new pathways to embed and strengthen – that's where your daily Purpose Primer comes in. By engaging with your newly formed beliefs, even for just five minutes each morning, you help to make these new pathways your default. Over time, this will free you from your past conditioning and enable you to fulfil your purpose.

Bringing it all together

Your beliefs have shaped every experience you've ever had. Some may have set you up for success, while others may have prevented you from fulfilling your potential. Until now, it's likely that much of this process has been unconscious but, now you're aware, you have the ability to free yourself from your old, limiting beliefs and replace them with empowering ones.

This enables you to venture into uncharted territory and go further than you'd previously believed possible. Each step that you take on this journey will be taken in the present moment, but many of us find ourselves lost in the worries that come with a busy life, held back by the past, or fearful of the future. How, then, can we drop these concerns and come fully into the present moment? Through mindfulness practise, which is where we go next.

Reflection

- What do you need to believe in order to fulfil your purpose?
- What beliefs do you think inspirational individuals, such as Rosa Parks or Mahatma Gandhi, held to make their impact possible?
- What is your key insight from this stage of your journey, and what will you do differently as a result?

STAGE FOUR

STEPPING INTO THE NOW

Mindfulness – where does the journey always unfold?

'Do not dwell in the past, do not dream of the future,
concentrate the mind on the present moment.'
Buddha

'Peace is every step. It turns the endless path to joy.'
Thich Nhat Hanh

As you travel the life-long journey that is fulfilment of purpose, you come to realise that your first step is as important as your last, and that nowhere you're heading is any more important than where you are right now. If you forget this, it's easy for every step you take to be considered simply a means to an end, leaving you frustrated by your slow progress and impatient to be further along the path. The unfortunate consequence of approaching your journey in such a way is that years of toil and resistance simply lead to more of the same, and the fruits of your labour never materialise. For you carve your path as you go: if you believe that you lack something now, then your present moment experience will be one of scarcity. Without a shift in consciousness, your future can only be experienced in the same way.

Indeed, there is a great paradox to your journey. While you now understand your purpose and have identified a series of associated goals that you've mapped out into the future, there is only ever *this* moment. A truly successful journey is one of balance: between creating a compelling future on the one hand, and never stepping out of the simplicity of the present moment on the other. For it is here, right now, that every idea arises, every plan is formulated, every action is taken, every accomplishment is achieved and every emotion is felt. *Everything* you're looking for, including the moment-by-moment fulfilment of your purpose, resides here in the now. It's crucial that you bridge the gap between your desired future and the present moment, removing the illusion that they are anything other than two sides of the same coin. Mindfulness is that bridge.

Why do we need mindfulness?

The world we now inhabit is almost unrecognisable to that our grandparents knew as children. Our modern lives are defined by an always-on culture, where the lines separating work and home life have been blurred, and screen-time, advertising and social media dominate our lives. The pace of change we're driving is unprecedented, and the strain is starting to show.

Stress levels have never been higher: in the UK alone, 17 million working days are lost to stress each year, at an estimated cost of £2.4

billion to the UK economy.[9] Many of us feel that we need alcohol to unwind at the end our working day, and the number of people requiring medication to overcome anxiety and depression continues to rise. We're struggling to cope with the demands of the modern world we've created, and every indicator suggests the pace of change is only going to increase. So, if we're already struggling to cope, and greater challenges lie ahead, doesn't it follow that we're heading for trouble?

Thankfully, this doesn't need to be our fate. We each have the most sophisticated tool in the known universe with which to adapt and evolve in the moment to our ever-changing environment: our minds.

Used correctly, your mind has the potential to handle every challenge posed by the modern world with relative ease. Used incorrectly, however, it can become an instrument that drives inner turmoil, breaks your sleep and creates ever-increasing spirals of worry and anxiety.

Mindfulness is the key to breaking these patterns. It's a way of being that allows you to use your mind optimally, in order to thrive. It's also the state of consciousness that serves as your gateway to inner peace and living in the moment. Drawing upon an example once shared by Eckhart Tolle, let's open up our understanding of mindfulness by looking at a holiday through the lens of two people: first Katy, who doesn't live mindfully, and then Anthony, who does.

The holiday

Katy has a busy job in the city and her stress levels are high. It's the middle of winter, and she feels she needs something to look forward to, in order to get through the coming months, so she books a holiday. As the weeks go by, Katy finds herself daydreaming about her summer holiday and unconsciously resists some of her work challenges as they arise. As the holiday approaches, she starts to put off work that can wait until she's back and feels desperate to get over the line.

After months of anticipation, the first day of the holiday finally arrives and Katy is in the taxi on the way to the airport with her family. However, rather than being in the moment, she's already thinking about checking-in and what she might need in duty free. Then, when she's on the flight, she's thinking about the hire car they need

---

9 Figures provided by the Mental Health Foundation: mentalhealth.org.uk.

to pick up at the other end and the mojito she'll be able to enjoy in the poolside bar. When they reach the hotel, she heads to the bar but, instead of being fully in the moment, finds herself already planning where they'll eat that night: the mojito is finished without her realising. When they arrive at the restaurant, instead of being there *fully*, she's already planning their activities, beginning with the beach the next day to unwind: her plate is empty, but she wasn't fully conscious of the meal she just ate.

On the beach, Katy finally gets the chance to lie down and awaits that magical feeling of relaxation and peace she's been striving for over the past few months. Instead, she finds it hard to switch off. Intrusive thoughts about work enter her head, so she shuts them out by losing herself in a book and then thinking about the evening's restaurant choice. This pattern continues for the next few days, as she struggles to unwind and feels frustrated by her inability to do so.

Day five of the ten-day break arrives and, for the first time, the momentum of Katy's mind has finally slowed. She feels fully present on the beach: feels the warmth of the sun on her skin, the sand beneath her feet and the exhilaration of stepping into cool water. A sense of deep peace arises within her, and Katy finally experiences what she has been waiting for since winter. This state of true wellbeing and inner harmony is fleeting, but she finds herself feeling more relaxed for the next couple of days.

However, Katy then becomes aware she's on day seven of her holiday. Her sense of inner peace recedes, and she begins to feel anxious about some of the work she put off and the full inbox awaiting her return. She still enjoys the last few days, but now regrets being unable to relax earlier. A sinking feeling kicks in on the last day and stays with Katy on her return home.

Katy's first day in the office sees her sense of wellbeing disappear within a matter of minutes, as the reality of her busy workload kicks in. She finds herself compelled to book another holiday, so she has something to look forward to once more, and so the pattern repeats.

Does Katy's experience resonate for you? Sadly, patterns like this play out for so many of us – and not just in relation to holidays. Our everyday lives are often out of sync with the present moment, meaning that when we do have the opportunity to relax, we find it impossible to stop the momentum of a mind that has been trained to strive for the future. How, then, might this same scenario play out if we live mindfully? Let's look at this now with Anthony, who has learned to live in the present moment.

Anthony also has a busy job in the city. However, he drops any resistance to this, understanding it's his choice to be there and instead simply actions his highest priority work in the moment. If he ever feels his workload is unmanageable, Anthony speaks to his manager *in the moment* and explores ways he could streamline or delegate some of his tasks. Alongside this proactive approach, Anthony still chooses to book a holiday, but this time not as a source of respite, but rather through the desire for a new experience. As his holiday approaches, rather than feeling desperate for the break, Anthony is excited, yet also undaunted by the prospect of returning to a workload that he's managing effectively.

On the day of departure, Anthony is fully present in the taxi with his family, talking about the trip and sharing his excitement. At the check-in desk he's *at* the check-in desk, making eye contact and connecting with the employee who serves him. On the plane, Anthony is present, choosing which in-flight entertainment he thinks he'll enjoy, while also engaging with his wife and children. At the hotel bar, Anthony relishes the fact they've arrived and celebrates with a mojito, tasting and cherishing every mouthful. He and his family are still free to plan their evening meal and activities for the week, but without ever forgetting that it's *here and now* they'll experience everything they're looking for.

On their first day on the beach, Anthony already experiences the feeling of the sun on his skin and the sound of the waves on the shore, because for the past few months he's been living life in alignment with the present moment. There's no momentum in his mind that needs to pass and he doesn't need to resync himself with the *now*. A deep background sense of peace and wellbeing arises within Anthony and continues throughout the holiday, as he cherishes each moment. As the holiday approaches its end, Anthony feels a natural sadness, which accompanies the end of any experience, but is still able to cherish the time he and his family have left.

When Anthony returns to his office desk, there's no inner resistance and no tasks that he has put off. He may choose to book another holiday, but only because he's keen to open up new experiences once more – not because he feels the need to escape his present reality.

How mindful are you?

Who do you currently identify with most: Katy or Anthony? Can you see that Anthony has simply learned how to live in the present moment and that Katy could easily do so, too? As you reflect, consider which path you choose going forwards in your own life.

Seven common misconceptions of mindfulness

There are seven common misconceptions of mindfulness that can prevent you from experiencing its full benefits. Let's clear some of these up quickly:

1. **Mindfulness is an escape from reality.** Rather than being an escape, mindfulness deepens your connection with reality. Instead of viewing the present moment through the filter of your past experience, you instead engage with it fully, unconditionally and objectively as it arises.

2. **Mindfulness is a tool to stop thinking.** Thinking happens; thoughts occur. Trying to stop thinking is like trying to stop breathing. Mindfulness doesn't free you from thoughts; it frees you from *identification* with thoughts. You no longer believe that, just because a thought has arisen, it must be valid or needs to be acted upon.

3. **Mindfulness is only practiced during meditation at the start or end of each day**. In fact, you could lead a fully mindful life without ever choosing to practise sitting meditation. Imagine you have blurry vision and have been given a perfect set of prescription glasses that allow you to see the world in 20/20 vision. You wouldn't set your alarm clock, head downstairs at the crack of dawn, sit for 15 minutes with the glasses on so you see the world perfectly, before taking them off and stumbling out of the door. Mindfulness gives you a new clarity of perception, so why would you choose to drop it during the day, when you need it most? Sitting meditation can, however, be invaluable as a way to both begin and deepen your practice, which we'll explore later.

4. **Mindfulness is a religious practice or belief system, or is in conflict with them**. Using the previous analogy, we would choose to wear a pair of prescription glasses whether we were Christian, Muslim, Buddhist or atheist, to ensure we see the world clearly, with no fear of this conflicting with our beliefs. Similarly, being able to experience precisely what is happening in the present moment through mindful attention enhances your experience of the world, without compromising any existing belief system.

5. **Mindfulness is a way of ignoring the 'negatives' in life**. In fact, one of the defining characteristics of mindfulness is non-judgmental attention. It's about moving beyond labels of 'good' or 'bad' and simply noticing what *is*. For example, you can be mindful of challenging thoughts and emotions triggered by the death of a loved one, just as you can be mindful of joyous thoughts and emotions on your wedding day. Crucially, acceptance is *not* the same as approval. Through mindfulness, you accept whatever arises in the present moment, without necessarily always wishing it was so.

6. **Mindfulness is only possible in a tranquil setting**. As a novice, practising mindfulness while walking in the woods can be much easier than on a busy commuter train, but the principles and results are the same. It's in challenging environments that your practise in more idyllic settings comes to the fore, helping to transform your ability to handle the pressures of our modern world.

7. **Mindfulness is a technique**. Rather than being a tool or technique, mindfulness is a way of being, which we'll explore in more detail now.

What is mindfulness?

In one of the clearest definitions available, Professor Jon Kabat-Zinn describes mindfulness as, 'The awareness that emerges through paying attention on purpose, in the present moment, and nonjudgmentally to the unfolding of experience moment by moment.'

So, mindfulness is a different level of awareness. A whole new way of seeing and interacting with your world. This is why practising mindfulness can transform the quality of your life without necessarily changing the content. However, even with this definition, mindfulness can still feel like an abstract concept that's difficult to pin down. We need to strip it back to basics to build our understanding. The core realisation to grasp is:

You are not your mind.

Nor are you your thoughts, emotions or the circumstances of your life.

So, who *are* you?

You are the one who has been able to consider your thoughts, feel your emotions, evaluate the circumstances of your life and steer your course. If life is a journey, then *you* are the adventurer.

If you were your mind, you wouldn't be able to differentiate between thoughts or choose different courses of action. For example, if you had the thought, 'I am in danger', it would be completely self-fulfilling. You wouldn't be able to see beyond it. This thought, rightly or wrongly, would simply be your reality. However, while you may have this thought in a particular situation – such as walking along a dark alley at night when you sense someone behind you – you have the capacity to observe, consider and, if appropriate, reframe it. For example, you might choose to think, 'It's possible that I might be in danger, but it's more likely that the person behind me is simply on their way home.' This revised thought will naturally have a knock-on impact on your emotional and biological response, determining whether you experience 'fight or flight', or remain calm.

So, *who* was it that was able to observe the thought as it entered your mind? *Who* was it that had the ability to choose whether to buy into it or reframe it, by creating a new thought? *That* was you. You have the capacity to observe what is happening in your world, both within (thoughts and emotions) and without (your environment), and to then use your mind to enact your chosen response, which determines the results you get. As such, you are a co-creator of your reality.

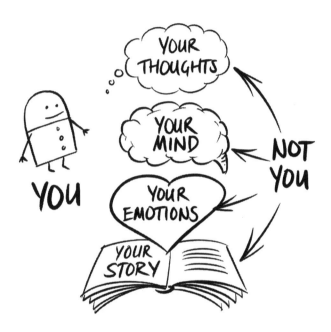

How mindfulness can transform your life

Mindfulness doesn't take away the 'negative' circumstances of your life, but you no longer make those circumstances part of who you view yourself to be. If you're experiencing the negative emotions associated with a job loss, that's what you're experiencing fully in the now. Conversely, if you're experiencing positive emotions associated with a job promotion, that's what you're experiencing fully in the now. In both scenarios, you're free to feel these emotions and to then choose your way forward. To respond rather than react. To choose not to believe in your imperfection in the first instance, nor in your greatness in the second. Rather, to realise that no external circumstance or outcome has the ability to affect your inner value. As such, you become the eye of the storm; the place of stillness and presence at the centre of whatever is unfolding in your life at any given moment.

The quality of your life will be defined by the choices you make in the present moment. For many of us, our actions are not so much a conscious choice as a reaction; we literally re-act an old subconscious thought-behaviour pattern. Some people go their whole lives in a reactive state, blaming the world for their internal struggles or the outer circumstances of their life while changing none of their behavioural choices. A life lived *on purpose*, on the other hand, sees you move from reaction to response. Through mindful attention, you notice the urge to react angrily when someone cuts you up in traffic, but choose to respond differently. You notice the desire to talk over somebody who expresses a viewpoint that differs from your own, but instead choose to respond by listening and asking questions, to broaden your perspective.

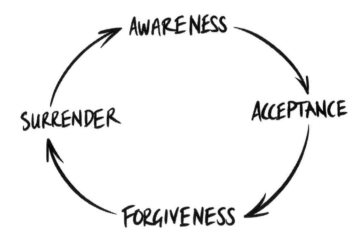

Moving from reaction to response is a moment by moment choice and a lifetime discipline. Each time someone or something in your environment triggers a reaction pattern, draw your conscious awareness to the urge to act, then pause for a moment and ask if this impulsive action will result in your desired outcome. If the answer is no, consciously choose a different path.

There are four key pillars that underpin the practice of mindfulness: awareness, acceptance, forgiveness and surrender. Relating this to the earlier example of a job loss, you allow yourself to be fully *aware* both of the situation and also of your automatic internal reaction, which is likely to include feelings of anxiety, anger or helplessness.

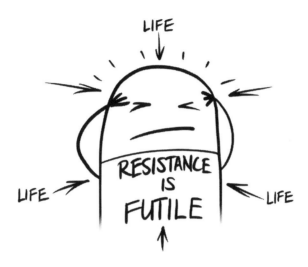

You then *accept* this present reality, knowing that resisting or denying the job loss (or the resulting emotions) won't change the situation and will in fact only keep you stuck. You understand on a fundamental level that resistance is futile. Again, it's important to clarify here that acceptance isn't the same as approval: it's perfectly natural for you to wish the situation was different, while still accepting it as reality. You also bring acceptance to the negative thoughts and emotions that have been automatically triggered, knowing that denying or repressing them will only prevent you from moving forwards.

Once you've brought your awareness and acceptance to the situation, you're now ready to *forgive*. Forgiveness frees you up and releases associated negative energy from your body. It's time to forgive everything that lies outside of your control, including the economy, your company policy, the role of your boss in the redundancy and your past mistakes (which are now in the past and therefore outside of your control).

Having freed up and released your past, you're now ready to *surrender* fully to the present moment and choose your path from this point. You may decide to evaluate whether this job was in fact *on purpose* for you and, if not, take some time to consider alternative paths. As such, living mindfully allows you to overcome life's challenges, learn valuable lessons and steer your course, all in the present moment.

Resistance is futile

A few years ago, on the way home from work, I was unexpectedly caught in a torrential downpour, the kind that only happens once or twice a year, where you're soaked through within a matter of seconds. I'd forgotten my umbrella and therefore found myself hunching my shoulders as I ran in search of somewhere I could shelter. I was in full resistance and denial mode, convincing myself that if I could run fast enough, I'd be able to avoid getting drenched. However, I was quickly forced to realise that my resistance was futile.

I was already wet through, my shoes were squelching and no action I could take would reverse this reality. At that precise moment, an interesting thing happened. I found myself taking a deep breath, my shoulders dropped from their hunched position, I slowed from a frantic run to a calm walk and I turned my face up to the sky, experiencing fully the exaltation of being struck by the rain. Simultaneously, I felt an enormous sense of inner peace and wellbeing arise within me.

This feeling of deep connection lasted for a couple of minutes, before being replaced by thoughts of how to best navigate my journey home, but my instinct told me I'd experienced something significant. I reflected upon the experience over the next few days, unsure how I could have had such a profoundly positive experience in a situation that, from the outside, seemed predominantly negative.

Unknowingly, I'd stumbled across the principle of surrender. No matter whether we deem our present circumstances to be positive or negative, when we drop all resistance and surrender, we experience a sense of connection and wellbeing. Since this discovery, I have experienced peace and contentment in my life whenever I remember to align with the present moment (which I still forget to do more than I'd like to admit!). I've also come to realise that peak experiences of joy, bliss and fulfilment result each time I combine this practice with total alignment with my values.

Let's explore whether this principle of surrender has already played out for you.

Your experience of surrender

Think about a time when you've experienced a sense of deep inner peace, contentment or connection – a peak memory, where everything felt in perfect balance and harmony, even if only for a few seconds. ↩

When you have this image in your mind, consider whether you had consciously or subconsciously surrendered to the present moment. If so, you've already experienced the power of surrender and the sense of connection that follows from this simple accomplishment.

If you can't recall a moment like this, consider whether you've ever truly surrendered to the present moment. What might have been holding you back? Experiment with dropping your resistance right now: simply allow yourself to sit in peace, surrendering to exactly where you are and to the fact there's nothing you need to do for the next couple of minutes. Do you feel a sense of peace stir within you?

How to practise mindfulness

The mindfulness and meditation exercises signposted below will help you to cultivate more peace and presence in your life going forwards. Before we begin, let me briefly share my own personal experience of mindfulness practice, to help get you thinking about what might work for you.

Practising mindfulness – in practice!

It's easy to read a book like this and assume the author wakes at 5am each day to head to a meditation studio, roll out a mat, assume the lotus position and sit contemplating the profound wonders of the universe for an hour, before repeating again in the evening after a day of calm serenity, interspersed with vegan wonders and Bikram Yoga. This, let's be clear, is *not* the case (not for me, anyway!).

Personally, I've found that carving out time for regular sitting meditation is a challenge. With a young family and a busy coaching practice, time is precious and energy a vital resource. I know from experience that getting up earlier than my usual 7am start would leave me short of energy, considering our daughter still wakes in the night and I often work in the evenings. Therefore, rather than retreating to a private space for meditation, I choose to enjoy being with my family in the morning, a time I find precious. I typically carve out a twenty-minute slot around 9am for meditation, which I try to honour regardless of how busy my diary is. The rest of my day is then packed with a combination of clients, writing, promotion, childcare and household chores, before the mayhem that is the kids' bedtime routine. I then continue to work with clients, write or read in the evening.

As you can see, there's not a lot of time for retreating to a meditation studio or sitting cross-legged in the woods, palms faced up to the universe! However, I wouldn't have it any other way. For me, this is a life fully lived. I choose to spend time with my children and I am fully present with them when I do. I choose to do work that I love and I am fully present as I do it. And I choose to carve out time for much-needed rest and relaxation whenever possible. I know the opportunity for more sitting meditation will come back as my children grow older but, for now, my mindfulness practice in the world is every bit as valuable.

While my current life circumstance and practice are unique to me, I wanted to share to illustrate that the mindfulness tools I'm making available aren't a requirement or prescription ↩

that you must follow. Everyone's life is unique and your path to practising mindfulness will be your own. Therefore, I encourage you to play, flex around your current life circumstances and see what works for you. Enjoy!

Beginning to practise mindfulness and meditation

The key to beginning your mindfulness practice is realising that your mind, and its associated senses, are the gateway to a mindful state of awareness. Think of any time you've had a cold shower, or waded into the cool sea on a hot day. You're shocked into the present moment and all past worries or future anxieties disappear in an instant. However, you don't need to overload or shock your senses to achieve a mindful state. By channelling your attention through your senses, you can draw your awareness into the here and now.

Imagine a typical workplace meeting. If you go into the meeting with a vague instruction to 'be mindful,' your mind won't know how to put this into practice. What exactly does 'be mindful' mean? And how will your mind know when it's off-track in order to course-correct? 'Stay in the moment' is slightly better, but still too broad to really be useful. So how can you programme your mind to bring about a mindful state? 'I choose to focus on *precisely* what's being said by whoever is speaking, as well as the meaning behind their words' gives your mind a laser focus. Quite simply, it's impossible to take in that level of information and not be fully present.

When it comes to meditation – the act of settling your mind and body into stillness – it's important to remember that the goal isn't to *stop* thinking. If you try to silence your mind, you'll likely experience frustration. Your aim is simply to allow whatever wants to arise to arise, including thoughts, but without engaging with or challenging them. By letting them be, you come to see them as separate to you, and a sense of spaciousness and inner peace arises.

These insights form the basis of each of the exercises below.

Practising mindfulness and meditation

By joining my community at *stevechamberlain.co.uk/livingonpurpose* you can access a free mindfulness and meditation guide to help you begin (or deepen) your practise. This includes tips on how to be mindful at work, while parenting and doing household chores, as well as some guided meditations. I invite you to choose one of the exercises and make a commitment to carving out ten minutes a day for one week. Notice how you feel before, during and after your practise, and whether you're more centred and present by the end of the week. Then explore the other exercises and include those that work for you within your daily priming ritual.

Obstacles and pitfalls

The mindful path is a simple one: live in the moment, accepting whatever arises before choosing your response. However, this doesn't necessarily mean it comes easily and personally, of everything covered in this journey, this is where I'm most likely to lose my way. There are five obstacles it's helpful to be aware of as you make your transition to a more mindful state of consciousness.

Obstacle one: time

> *'There is a time to live and a time to die,*
> *but never to reject the moment.'*
> **Lao Tzu**

The first obstacle you're likely to come across is time. It's easy to think you don't have time to practise mindfulness, or that you'll begin to practise when life quietens down. But mindfulness is always practised now and there's never a time that's not now. It was now when you were born, when you took your first step and when you graduated from school. It was now when you first picked up this book and when you finish reading it, it will be now. The day you die – and every moment in between – will be now.

It doesn't take any time to practise mindfulness, in the same way that it doesn't take any time to wear prescription glasses. Mindfulness is simply a way of engaging with the world. Depending upon the circumstance on any given day, you may not always have time for sitting practice, but you have infinite time in which to practise moment-by-moment mindfulness: an infinity of now.

Your experience of time

Take a moment to consider if there has ever been a time in your life when it wasn't now, or if there will ever be a point in the future when it won't be now.

Ultimately, there's no such thing as time, but in a practical day-to-day sense, time is invaluable. You've used your values and purpose to determine your future goals, and their realisation in a future now will be what transforms your world for the better. Therefore, it's still crucial that you map out the future you wish to see and the steps that it will take to get there. But simultaneously, never lose sight of the fact that each step will be taken in the present moment, and everything you're looking for – including the wisdom to guide you – will be experienced in the present moment. As such, you can think of time as a tool you can use on your journey, much as you use your values as a compass. Living *on purpose* means understanding and embracing this paradox as you chart and live your life on the line.

Obstacle two: it's not as simple as it sounds

> *'Everything is hard before it is easy.'*
> **Johann Wolfgang von Goethe**

The concept of living life in the present moment sounds incredibly simple – and it is. However, for the majority of us, it's not how we've lived our lives until this moment. As you begin your practice, mindfulness can feel much more difficult than you expected, leading to feelings of frustration and doubts that it can, in fact, lead to the inner peace you've been promised.

To help understand why this plays out, it's useful to think about the process that unfolds every time you try something new. There are four key learning stages that you go through, as conceptualised by Noel Burch in the 1970s.

Initially you're in a state of *unconscious incompetence*. You don't yet know that you don't know how to do something, so there's no sense of frustration or stress. Taking learning to drive as an example, unconscious incompetence would be the point before you've ever chosen to get behind the wheel of a car. You don't know how to drive, but it causes you no anxiety because you don't know how hard it is or where your failings lie; you're in blissful ignorance!

The next stage is *conscious incompetence*. At this point, you become acutely aware of the fact that you aren't yet proficient at a new skill. This would be the equivalent of the first time you try to find the clutch biting point in a manual car, but you keep stalling. Even though you're further down the line than you were at stage one, you're actually more uncomfortable now.

After an extended period of practice, failure, success and learning, you reach the stage of *conscious competence*. At this point, you know how the clutch works and can find the biting point without stalling almost all of the time. However, it still takes conscious effort and you're not yet able to do it on autopilot.

The final stage arrives after a longer period of practice and application, where you finally reach *unconscious competence*, also known as mastery. At this point, you can find the biting point without even thinking about it, and you're able to talk to others in the car while effortlessly pulling away and changing gears. Once you reach this final stage, you're back to the same sense of ease that you had within unconscious incompetence, but this time you've internalised your new skill.

If you haven't come across mindfulness before, you'll likely now find yourself at stage two – conscious incompetence (otherwise known as the infuriating stage!). As you begin your practice for the first time, you become aware of how little of your life you currently spend in the present moment and how much time you're lost in thought. You may also realise how little control you currently have over your mind. The natural result is a sense of discomfort and frustration. It was actually easier to be at stage one, where you were blissfully unaware of your disconnection with the present moment. However, as with anything you've ever learned, this is part of the process; you cannot skip a stage. By staying in the game, and allowing yourself to accept and forgive any frustration that arises, the process of learning to practise mindfulness becomes mindfulness practice in and of itself.

Obstacle three: it's too unscientific

*'Time is not at all what it seems. It does
not flow in only one direction, and the future exists
simultaneously with the past.'*
Albert Einstein

Does some of this mindfulness content seem unscientific or too 'spiritual' for you? Depending upon your belief system, this could lead you to resist some of the insights, or hold back from choosing to live mindfully, for fear it's not based on 'sound' principles.

However, there's a compelling scientific basis for mindfulness, which is why it has medical backing and is recommended by many health professionals as a means of managing conditions such as anxiety and depression. The cutting-edge field of quantum physics also now proves the core underlying principle to be true: time is not how we experience it through our senses. Indeed, much of the work of Einstein was based on this insight. His theory of relativity shows that time does not objectively exist, and only becomes a reality because of our perception. For example, if nothing existed in our universe, and there was no observer, time would simply cease to exist. There would just be space, or pure potential. Even with one point in space, time still does not exist. However, as soon as a second point is added, our concept of time is created. There is now a distance to be travelled between the two objects and the time it takes for this to happen.

Einstein also proved mathematically that, were we to travel fast enough, we could arrive at our destination before we left – something that is inconceivable to our senses (and that still makes my head spin to think about!). We also now know that time is experienced fundamentally differently close to the surface of a black hole as compared to earth, with one year equating to many hundreds of years on earth. Such findings don't compute with our personal experience, yet are now proven and accepted models within the field of quantum physics. Einstein was led to conclude that 'the distinction between past, present and future is only a stubbornly persistent illusion.'

So, far from being unscientific, mindfulness points to a fundamental truth: that time is a human concept, and that past and future as we know them do not exist 'out there'. The present moment is all there is. The now is where every idea in history has been conceived, where every action has been taken and where everything we're looking for resides. Mindfulness gets us back in touch with the only place that truly exists: the here and now, where life always has – and always will – unfold.

Obstacle four: subconscious fear of the present moment

'You must live in the present, launch yourself on every wave, find your eternity in each moment.'
Henry David Thoreau

Up until this moment, it's possible that you've experienced 'now' as a scary place. Depending upon your past, it may be where you've had to face chronic or acute anxiety, fear, guilt, violence or abuse. Similarly, when you turn on the news, you're met with a seemingly never-ending stream of shocking events and acts of cruelty taking place right 'now'. It's therefore natural that, on a subconscious level, we sometimes fear stepping fully into the present moment.

Client case study – Alexandra

Several years ago, in one of our coaching sessions, Alexandra mentioned a dream she'd had. She was standing on a boat looking down into crystal clear, calm water that she felt compelled to jump into. But despite a deep instinct that the water was safe, something stopped her, and she instead found herself pulled in the other direction. As we explored what this water might represent, it became apparent that it was a symbol for the now, or life itself, which always unfolds in the now and is therefore inseparable from it. In our preceding session she shared that she viewed the world as a dangerous place and therefore *never* lived in the present moment. Her dream seemed to be her subconscious mind telling her that, despite her fears, it was a safe place to go. However, Alexandra had been verbally and physically abused by her father as a child and had learned from an early age that the present moment was a place fraught with danger. We needed to explore which possibility represented the truth.

First, I asked Alexandra to imagine herself as an objective bystander of her life over the past five years. She was to imagine that she had a clipboard, and each moment of every day she was to mark a red cross each time there was genuine danger (crucially, not simply a *perceived* danger) and to mark a blue cross each moment the outer environment was safe. Viewed from this dispassionate position, she realised there was not a single red mark across the whole five years, while the blue marks were seemingly infinite. This exercise alone led to a shift, as she suddenly realised the fear she had been experiencing was in her own head and not, as she'd believed, in the world. She had disappeared into the world of thought as a child to protect herself from genuine danger, but for the rest of her life she had remained lost there, resulting in her experiencing the same fears day after day. The present moment had genuinely felt like a perilous place, but only because she believed her thoughts.

Next, we explored the news, which seemingly confirmed her view that the world was a dangerous place. Again, I asked her to become an objective bystander, and to consider whether the news was a balanced reflection of events. To do so, I asked her whether the tragedy of a homicide would be deemed newsworthy; she agreed this was likely to make the headlines. I then asked her how many other people, on the same night the homicide took place, would have been safely asleep in bed. Her answer? Millions. The difference being that these millions of positive stories are simply not deemed newsworthy.

For the first time in her adult life, these insights freed Alexandra up to step into the crystal clear water of the present moment.

If we believe the present moment is dangerous, then it makes perfect sense that we won't want to step into it. Coming into the now of our worst fears, or the present moment as depicted in the news, would feel like jumping into shark-infested waters. However, once we realise these old, unconscious thoughts aren't valid, and that the present moment actually represents clear, safe, tranquil water, we're free to immerse ourselves in it. Even when negative events play out, we understand that years of staying on the boat in fear won't actually protect us from them, and that we can handle anything that comes our way. Once we experience the beauty and simplicity of the now, we'll never choose to climb back into the false safety of the boat again.

Obstacle five: a belief that mindfulness solves everything

'If there's only one answer, then this must
not be a very interesting topic.'
Ron Jeffries

The final trap it's easy to fall into is that mindfulness solves everything. It doesn't. If you hate your job, you'll still experience painful thoughts and feelings associated with this. If you believe, subconsciously, that you're inferior to others or that the world is a scary place, you'll still suffer. But you won't be lost in your thoughts and feelings as you were before, and will therefore be empowered to change your choice of direction or your beliefs. This is why mindfulness is a stage on your journey, no more or less important than the others. When you're off track, mindfulness allows you to become conscious of what has taken you there and to course-correct, by focusing on your values, purpose, beliefs, mindset and skillset in the present moment. Once you've realigned your life, you then experience feelings of joy, peace and fulfilment in the now through the same mindful attention. In this way, mindfulness is not the sole answer to your problems, but rather a vital part of the whole.

Bringing it all together

Each time you choose to step into the present moment, you are being mindful. Each time you forget and become lost in thoughts of the past or future, you lose yourself again. However, the door is never closed. You *always* have that choice and, as your practice deepens, you learn to use time to remember and to plan, while still residing in the perfection of the present moment.

If you take one thing away from this stage of your journey, let it be that mindfulness is simply a return to your true nature. All animals on this planet, other than humans, live in eternal mindfulness, and we too experience this state whenever we drop the illusion of past and future, and return to the simplicity of 'now'. After all, life is the journey, not the destination, and the journey always unfolds exactly where you are.

Reflection

- Right now, do your emotions tell you that you're living *on purpose*?
- Can you sense you're able to handle anything that arises here, in the simplicity of the present moment?
- What is your key insight from this stage of your journey, and what will you do differently as a result?

STAGE FIVE

OVERCOMING OBSTACLES
AND CHALLENGES

Mindset – what if you could handle anything?

'I've missed more than 9,000 shots in my career. I've lost almost 300 games. Twenty-six times I've been trusted to take the game winning shot and missed. I've failed over and over and over again in my life. And that is why I succeed.'
Michael Jordan

'The only person you are destined to become is the person you decide to be.'
Ralph Waldo Emerson

Our journey is now well underway and, through mindfulness, you're beginning to realise that there's only ever one step for you to take: the one you're taking in this moment. However, as you travel further into previously uncharted territory, you're likely to experience new challenges. Obstacles that you hadn't previously foreseen appear to block your way and you need to adapt your approach in order to move forwards. In fact, living *on purpose* typically calls you to higher ground and, therefore, more challenging terrain. It's your mindset that enables you to persist in the face of such challenges and to continue your ascent.

Developing a winning mindset is crucial to living *on purpose,* as it enables you to build unshakeable confidence, resilience and self-worth, freeing you up to step into your full potential. Let's begin by exploring what mindset is, before giving you the opportunity to consciously strengthen your own.

What is mindset?

Mindset is the way in which you engage your mind to approach a challenge or goal: how you *set* your *mind* to achieve a desired outcome. Until now, your mindset may have come about by chance, dependent perhaps upon your mood, the task at hand or your belief system. Now you know your mind is a tool you can use to help you achieve your purpose, you're able to consciously carve out the optimal mindset for any situation. And given that your mind is the most powerful known tool in the universe, the results can be remarkable.

There are two key stages to understanding how to cultivate an optimal mindset: the first is understanding how the mind works; the second is knowing how to programme it.

How the mind works

The mind operates in broadly the same way for everyone. While we each have our own personality and idiosyncrasies, each of our minds essentially functions using the same operating system, and the results we achieve are largely determined by the programming we put into it. Your thoughts and beliefs, as well as the questions you ask, form this programming and trigger corresponding emotions in the body. Your emotions then drive your behaviour. Crucially, *you* are the programmer.

In this way, you can think of your thoughts and emotions as the heads and tails on a coin: you can't have the heads without the tails, in the same way that you can't have a thought without a corresponding emotional reaction within your body. If you think a happy thought, you experience happiness and act accordingly. If you think an anxious thought, you experience anxiety and behave accordingly. You may not always be aware of the thought that triggered the emotion, but you will *feel* it. In much the same way, your emotional state can influence your thinking. For example, if you're experiencing toxic emotions, such as anger or fear, you're much more likely to have negative thoughts than if you're experiencing positive emotions, such as happiness or gratitude.

YOUR JOURNEY

The mind-body connection

To experience the relationship between your mind and body, try holding yourself small, hunching your shoulders, dropping your chin, adopting a negative facial expression and ↩

breathing shallowly. How do you feel? How creative and expansive are your thoughts likely to be? Now, sit up tall, drop your shoulders back and down, take a deep breath and smile. How do you feel? What is possible for you from this place?

Your body, then, can create ease or tension within your mind, and your thoughts can create ease or tension within your body. From this foundation, let's explore seven insights that will help you understand how your mind works.

1. Your mind is perfect and neutral

At first glance, this insight might seem an *impossible* assertion. Many of us experience our mind as *anything* but perfect and neutral, and may even view it as our own worst enemy. It wakes us at 2am worrying about a performance appraisal at work the next day, or ruminates endlessly on something that happened in the past, causing chronic stress and anxiety. However, your mind is not an adversary. If you look more closely, you'll realise it's *always* trying to serve you, even when your experience may seem far from this reality. It won't wake you at 2am unless you've told it – consciously or unconsciously – that there's something for you to be fearful of in the appraisal, or if you instinctively know you haven't done enough preparation; and it will only rehash past events if you haven't fully processed them[10].

Your mind is perfect, neutral and here to serve you. Much like a genie in a lamp, your mind will aim to grant your every wish, but you need to be careful what you wish for. Like the fable of King Midas, who wished for everything he touched to be turned to gold, only to find he then couldn't eat or drink, your mind will do *precisely* what you ask it to do, without question. There is no negative intent behind its actions, for it is *neutral*; if you get bad results, it's simply because you haven't yet programmed your mind correctly. And that's because no one has ever shown you how.

---

10 Refer to the steps of awareness, acceptance, forgiveness and surrender in the mindfulness chapter.

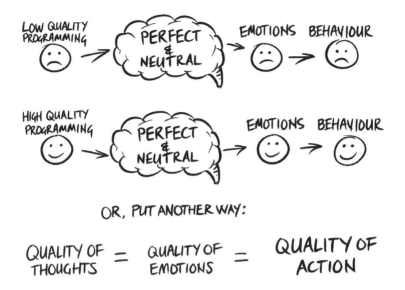

To illustrate, if you asked your mind to tell you all of the ways in which you're inadequate, it will dutifully delve into its memory bank, before comparing you to everyone you view as superior: your Ford Focus suddenly looks like a sorry excuse for a car compared with your friend's Porsche; your parenting skills fall short of your neighbour's, who gladly home schools; and your golf handicap suddenly looks appalling when compared with Rory McIlroy! You could easily claim your mind is your worst enemy in this circumstance, but in reality, it has given you the *perfect* answer to the question you've asked and, as such, has served you dutifully.

If you rewind and ask the opposite question, your mind will search its databank for examples where you excel. To do so, it will compare you against more favourable yardsticks, so suddenly, your Ford Focus looks fantastic compared with your previous clapped-out banger; you recognise you're constantly learning and evolving as a parent; and your golfing skills stack up pretty well when compared with many of your friends. This is the same perfect and neutral mind. The only thing that's changed is the question you asked: the quality of your programming.

2. Subconscious programming is still programming

This is where our earlier work on beliefs was so crucial. Because if you still hold subconscious beliefs that don't serve you, your mind will automatically assume they are valid. For example, if you hold a subconscious and unexamined belief that you're stupid, your mind will still draw upon this as an important piece of information. When job searching, you might ask, 'What kind of jobs should I apply for?' But your mind will use this pre-programmed belief to filter the question, so it will instead ask, 'Knowing that I'm not very clever [subconscious belief], what kind of jobs should I apply for?' The answer to these two questions may be markedly different, potentially stopping you from applying for stimulating jobs you would thrive in.

This is why you need to be *absolutely* clear on your beliefs, and to think carefully about the questions you ask your mind. In the above example, your mind is again trying to serve you, but simply doesn't know the difference between a conscious and subconscious belief, or between fact and fiction.

3. Your conscious mind can only focus on one thing at a time

While your mind can flit incredibly quickly from thought to thought, it cannot think two things simultaneously. This means that by consciously directing your attention onto thoughts, emotions and behaviours that you desire, you cannot also experience other unwanted states. To illustrate, let's imagine you're currently feeling anxious. To overcome this, you simply draw your attention to things that are safe in your present environment. In response to the question, 'What is safe here?' your mind will automatically serve you by noticing the walls around you that are solid; the roof over your head that's designed to protect you from the elements; the friendly people in your field of vision, and so on. In so doing, you've stepped out of anxiety simply through conscious attention.

The questions you ask your mind, therefore, help to determine where your mind focuses, and the way a question is worded directly influences the answer generated. For example, if you ask, 'What might go wrong?' before taking a decision, your mind will dutifully provide you with a raft of worst-case scenarios, as well as triggering associated anxiety-inducing thoughts. If, on the other hand, you ask, 'What's my ideal outcome and how can I make this my reality?' your mind will come back with positive scenarios, triggering correlated thoughts and emotions. In this way, alongside your thoughts and beliefs, the questions you ask form part of the programming. If you want to experience an extraordinary life, it's imperative that you begin to ask higher-quality questions.

4. Your mind will always try to protect you

Your mind's core function is to ensure your survival. As such, it has evolved to be hypersensitive to potential threats in your environment – but it cannot differentiate between real versus perceived threats. It relies upon *you* to make that distinction. For example, if you're about to walk into a job interview and you tell your mind that interviews are *terrifying*, your mind will trust you implicitly. It will perceive this to be a dangerous situation and do everything it can to protect you from threat. That means scanning the environment for sources of danger, including negative facial expressions from your interviewers, as well as answering questions defensively if it perceives they are exposing your weaknesses. Your mind will also trigger your fight or flight response in the face of any perceived threats – a crucial strategy for survival in our ancestral past but, in this scenario, the exact opposite of your ideal state.

5. Your mind cannot *not* go somewhere

This heading is confusing for a reason: it's hard to process. Which is likely to be the same as some of the programming you currently give your mind. Let's imagine you've recently been experiencing a growing state of anxiety at work, which you no longer wish to be the case. What might you typically say to yourself as you approach the office on Monday morning? 'I don't want to be stressed today.' There's a logic to this, but it's faulty programming.

To illustrate, imagine you get into your car to go on a day trip to Edinburgh Castle. You get out your Sat Nav to enter the destination. At this point, you wouldn't type in 'Not Dover Castle' or any other attractions you *don't* want to visit, because you understand that your

Sat Nav needs to be told where *to go*, not where *not* to go. You type in 'Edinburgh Castle', so your Sat Nav can serve you.

Your mind is like a complex computer. It computes data and, much like a Sat Nav, it has no idea what to do when you tell it where you *don't* want it to go, or what you *don't* want it to do. What can your mind do when you programme it with, 'Don't worry'? It will try to serve you, but it doesn't know what the outcome should look or feel like, as you are seeking an *absence* of something: you've created a broken feedback loop. Ironically, this creates a sense of anxiety: by trying to avoid worry, you've actually created more of it. In addition, by not wanting to feel stressed, you've unwittingly programmed your mind to seek out potential sources of stress in your environment, so it can then protect you from them. In doing so, you're drawing your attention to the negative factors in your environment rather than the positive, which will again increase your anxiety.

6. Your mind loves clear and simple programming

Building on the above insight, your mind loves simple programming. For example, if I ask you to spot something green in your environment, you'll see something almost instantly, because your mind understands the instruction and can action it immediately. However, we often unwittingly use confusing or unnecessarily complicated programming. For example, if you feel anxious before going to a party, you might say to yourself, 'I just want to seem normal.' Your mind has no idea what *normal* is, so in trying to serve you, it will scan your environment to see what other people are doing and then attempt to imitate, making you feel insincere and awkward. You're likely to have a bad experience and may then conclude that you're *not* 'normal', when in fact it was just that your programming was too vague.

The key to optimal programming is to determine your desired outcome and then set your mind an intention that will help you achieve your goal. For example, using the party scenario once more, if your ideal outcome is to feel engaged and present, your intention might be, 'To talk to some interesting people.' This gives you a clear external focus and allows much of your self-consciousness and anxiety to drop away[11]. The ideal programming will be different for each of us and depend upon the situation at hand, but the clarity and simplicity of your intention is the key.

7. Your mind is an evaluating, not decision-making, machine

When faced with a decision, such as whether to stay in your current job or move to a different role, you may initially ask your mind to list the pros and cons of each course of action. Your mind has evolved perfectly to perform evaluative tasks like this and duly obliges. However, if you then ask, 'What should I do?' the problems will kick in. Your mind will sift through all the available information to make the best possible logical decision, as instructed. If you happen to have had a great day at work when you ask it to decide, your logical mind will take this into account and be more likely to conclude that staying is the best option. If, on the other hand, you've just had a terrible day, it's likely to decide it's time to hand in your notice. Similarly, your mind will process the question differently depending on whether you've just read an article about someone who took a career risk and is now reaping the rewards, or one about the economic downturn and subsequent looming job crisis.

If you ask, 'What should I do?' there's an assumption that your mind is who *you* are, and it can therefore make the decision. But it's not who you are: it's a tool that you use. Posing this question is the equivalent of asking your Sat Nav, 'Which attraction shall I visit today?' Your Sat Nav is, of course, simply a computer and therefore has no preference, so this question is nonsensical; it's on *you* to decide. And so it is with your mind: *you* are here to make the decision – by aligning with your values and purpose – and your mind is the tool you use to inform and execute that decision.

---

11 Naturally, your belief system will also impact here. If you believe you have nothing interesting to say (subconscious programming), then your intention will be undermined. Therefore, each of these insights work together.

Client case study — Viktor

When Viktor contacted me, I sensed the urgency behind his request for coaching. We managed to find a slot at short notice and, at the start of our session, Viktor told me he was worried he might be losing his mind. In the past week, completely out of the blue and for the first time in his life, he had suffered two panic attacks. He'd since seen his doctor, who had prescribed anxiety-inhibiting drugs, but Viktor was concerned about taking long-term medication and wanted to see if there was another way.

At the start of our session, I intentionally asked what must have sounded like a daft question: 'Do you believe your mind is perfect and neutral?' Unsurprisingly, he laughed and replied, 'Anything but!' I asked him to hold this new theory lightly and that we would explore it together. Next, I asked him to reveal the circumstances of his first panic attack. It had occurred the day after an end-of-year celebration with some of his postgraduate university classmates. He didn't normally drink and wasn't used to being hungover. He said that the following morning, when alone in his flat, he noticed feeling shaky and disconnected. This marked the onset of the attack, and over the next couple of hours it had developed into a full-blown panic attack, with heart palpitations, sweating and dizziness.

Having experienced panic attacks in my past, I understood that, no matter how scary they may feel, they're simply the natural result of faulty programming. I asked what thoughts had arisen when he noticed his initial symptoms (which we speculated may have been the natural signs of a hangover). He identified thoughts including, 'What's going on?', 'I don't like this feeling' and 'How can I stop this?' These thoughts unwittingly programmed his mind to turn inwards and become hypersensitive to the sensations in his body. They also programmed it to see these sensations as 'bad' and something to be stopped.

But energy can't be stopped, it can only be channelled. As a result of being energised by this additional focus and internal resistance, the sensations grew stronger and, much like a Jack In The Box, the pressure built. By this point, Viktor reported feeling a sense of overwhelm and new thoughts, including, 'Am I losing control?' and 'Am I going mad?' arose. His perfect and neutral mind did its best to answer, this time conjuring images of what it might look like to be losing control and 'going mad'. This fuelled the whirlwind of anxiety and toxic energy in his body which, by now, had reached such a level that it needed to be released. The mind and body did this in the only way it knew how: via heart palpitations, shaking and sweating – all symptoms of a panic attack.

By the time of his second panic attack, Viktor was primed to scan for warning signs that he was losing control again. He had unwittingly put himself into a hypervigilant state, where normal bodily sensations and emotions were put under excessive scrutiny and interpreted negatively. Not only did this trigger the start of a second panic attack, but also meant it escalated much more quickly than the first.

During our session together – and now with a clear understanding of how the panic attacks were unwittingly self-created – Viktor visibly dropped his shoulders, took a deep breath and smiled as the insight landed. Rather than ↵

being a sign of 'going mad', both panic attacks actually showed his mind was working perfectly. We closed our session with some mindful breathing techniques, to give Viktor a way to release excess energy from his body when needed. He sent me the following message a few weeks later:

'I just wanted to say I'm very grateful for our session. Now that I understand the mechanics of anxiety, I've seen a massive improvement. My feelings of panic have completely disappeared.'

Viktor's story is a sign that perfection and imperfection coexist. It was of course undeniably *imperfect* to have a panic attack. In fact, it was one of the worst experiences of his life. But paradoxically, it was also the *perfect* result of the quality of programming going through his mind at the time. There was nothing wrong with Viktor's mind. It was simply the programming that needed to change. Without this insight, he could have been on prescription drugs for months, years even, and could feasibly have believed there was something fundamentally wrong with him, all as a result of a simple misunderstanding of how the mind works.

The Sky+ Box analogy

To help pull together the above insights and deepen your understanding of who you are in relation to your mind, let's use a Sky+ or TiVo box as an analogy. Bring to mind a relative who struggles with technology and imagine that, for their birthday, you've given them a Sky+ Box but didn't have time to show them how it works or give them the instruction manual. When you next visit a few weeks later, rather than being grateful as you expected, they are frustrated: they've been trying to record their favourite TV programme – *The Great British Bake Off* – but keep on getting *Love Island* instead, much to their annoyance!

You ask them to show you what they've been doing and soon realise they're pressing the wrong series of buttons on the remote. So, what do you do? Do you call up Sky to report that the box is faulty? Do you shout at the box? Do you get angry with your relative?

Of course, the answer is *none of the above*. You instead teach them the correct way to program the machine. The instant you program the Sky+ box correctly, it gives you the results you want. The box doesn't say, 'Hang on, you've been programming me incorrectly for the last few weeks, so I won't change the output for another couple of months.' The change is *instant*.

How does this relate to your mind? In this analogy, you are the relative; the Sky+ Box is your mind; and the buttons being pressed on the remote control is the programming you put into it (your thoughts, beliefs and the questions you ask). Just as there was nothing wrong with your relative, so too there's nothing wrong with *you* – you've just never been shown how to correctly program your mind. And just as the Sky+ Box was perfect, neutral and waiting to be programmed in the optimal way, so it is with your mind. If you persist in holding untrue and unhelpful beliefs, giving negative thoughts your attention, or asking low-quality questions, you'll continue to get low-quality results. If, however, you move to true and helpful beliefs, focus on positive thoughts and start asking high-quality questions (using the remote control in the optimal way), then your mind will give you high-quality results, instantly.

Over the years, you may have lambasted your mind, even claiming it's your own worst enemy. You may even believe you've been given a faulty mind (the equivalent of a broken Sky+ Box). However, if you could switch your mind with that of a genius, such as Einstein, but then continued to program it exactly as you do now, you'd get the same output. Einstein wasn't a genius because of his mind, but because of his profound understanding of how the mind works and the optimal questions/programming it requires. Indeed, Einstein once stated, 'If I had an hour to solve a problem and my life depended on the solution, I would spend the first 55 minutes determining the proper question to ask, for once I know the proper question, I could solve the problem in less than five minutes.' Einstein understood on a fundamental level that the quality of the question (programming) determines the quality of the answer (output).

How long does it take to change faulty programming?

Of course, while your mind is, at its core, perfect and neutral, the existing programming may be anything but. We all have unconsciously adopted beliefs and patterns of thinking, and inevitably some of this may prove to be low-quality programming. This will be particularly true if you've had a challenging childhood. For example, a person with an alcoholic or abusive parent is likely to have a lot of faulty programming in place. This is the equivalent of inheriting a second-hand Sky+ Box, complete with all the old 'series records' for negative, violent or abusive shows. If this person has never been told they have the option to reprogramme the box, these shows will continue to play out for a lifetime. But this doesn't mean their machine is broken; as soon as they're given the remote and shown how to use it, they'll be empowered to delete the old programmes and change the output.

Your programming isn't hardwired and can be changed with conscious effort. Depending upon your past, this may involve working with a highly skilled therapist or coach, or you may choose to follow the steps outlined here to do so. Either way, time, compassion and patience will be needed as you replace the old programming and begin to embed new beliefs and patterns of behaviour. The moment you think empowering thoughts, you'll be rewarded with positive emotions; any time you slip back into old, disempowering thinking habits, your familiar toxic emotions will return. It can take time and conscious effort to build new thinking habits, yet there is *no* time involved in experiencing different results when you do so. Initially, stepping into new thinking habits may feel unfamiliar, like watching a new TV show for the first time, but in time you'll realise that those old negative recordings, to which you may have been addicted, weren't who you are. In fact, they created unnecessary fear and drove unhelpful behaviour.

Through this process, you create new neural pathways in your mind and, in time, the old pathways that are no longer firing degrade and fall away: you are literally reprogramming your mind.

How to programme your mind

Let's now look at some ways in which you can hone your programming, by consciously creating your mindset.

Cultivate a growth mindset

In her excellent book, *Mindset*, Professor Carol Dweck outlines the importance of developing a *growth* rather than *fixed* mindset. We're all born with a growth mindset. As a toddler, when we're learning to walk but fall over for the fiftieth time, we don't yell, 'I'm useless at walking, I quit!' thereby dooming ourselves to a lifetime of crawling to social events and important board meetings. However, as we grow older, many of us develop a fixed mindset in relation to certain areas of our lives. We may decide we're terrible at remembering names; that we're a poor public speaker; or that we're good but not great at inspiring others. Crucially, once we adopt a fixed mindset, we determine that we can't get better than our current level of proficiency, meaning we no longer make efforts to improve. Dweck's comprehensive research shows that a fixed mindset holds us back both from fulfilling our potential and enjoying the process. The good news is, it doesn't have to be this way.

Some of us manage to maintain a growth mindset throughout our lives. We trust that we're able to improve our abilities given time, practice and appropriate support. We see mistakes and hard work as part of our journey to mastery and keep going, just as we did when learning to take our first steps. Dweck's work highlights that a growth mindset is a crucial factor in our success in life and, just as importantly, that it's something we can consciously cultivate.

Moving from a fixed to a growth mindset

Bring to mind any areas in your life in which you'd ideally like to excel in order to live fully *on purpose*, but believe your current capabilities are set in stone and would therefore be hard to improve. You can use the following prompts to help identify any fixed mindset beliefs:

- I'll never be good at...
- I can't get any better at...
- I could never excel at...

Next, consider areas in which you are proficient, be it reading, writing, cooking, swimming, or any other talent, and consider how long it took to build your skillset. Do you remember the frustration or strain as you struggled to grasp the basics or reach the next level? Do you take these skills for granted now and forget the effort it took to acquire them? Is it possible that if you put the same time and effort (in the case of learning to read and write, many years) into improving your desired skill, you'd notice considerable improvement? How much do you want to improve your chosen skill?

If, upon reflection, it's important to you – and the fulfilment of your purpose – that you improve in this area, add the following belief to your Purpose Primer:

'Given time and dedication, I can improve my [insert area of focus] skills, and I choose to do everything within my power to achieve mastery in this field.'

We'll come onto the specifics of how you can accelerate your skill development in the next stage of our journey but, for now, trust that you have the capability to broaden your skillset if you adopt a growth mindset and are willing to put in the work.

Harness the power of semantics

Everything we think and say is programming. *Everything*. It's therefore crucial that we become conscious of what we say and how we say it, if we wish to achieve extraordinary results in our lives.

Let's bring this to life with the words *should* and *could*. Two similar looking and sounding words, yet the impact of using one over another can be profound. Consider the sentences below, which you might easily say to yourself at the start of a busy working day:

- I *could* clear my inbox today
- I *should* clear my inbox today

The emotional tone of each of these statements is markedly different. In the first instance, *could* implies possibility and choice. In the second, *should* implies obligation and an external standard to which you must adhere. Imagine now that an unforeseen work crisis arises, and your manager instructs you to drop everything you'd been planning to do today to prioritise its resolution. You work flat-out all day and manage to avert the crisis when you shut down your computer at 9pm. How do you feel? This depends on the language you used at the start of the day. If you used the word *could*, you probably feel proud of your work and vindicated in deprioritising your inbox. If, on the other hand, you used *should*, you're likely to experience a background sense of guilt or dissatisfaction at having not completed what you originally set out to achieve, even though you've worked hard all day and are leaving the office beyond your contracted hours.

The difference here was a single word, but the impact is huge. It's the same for many other words in our vocabulary. Consider the following:

- I *have* to do the cleaning
- I *choose* to do the cleaning

- I *must* pay the bills
- I *plan to* pay the bills

- I *need* to get back to that client
- I *intend* to get back to that client

The wording in the first of each of these examples is rigid and opens the possibility of failure. The second puts us at the point of control and is flexible, making us feel more motivated and empowered.

THEIR JOURNEY

Client case study – Natasha

Natasha was a single parent in her late thirties, with a high-pressured job in a global corporation and an eleven-year-old daughter who was about to start secondary school. Natasha had experienced a volatile and challenging upbringing with an alcoholic parent and was starting to notice similar conflict patterns developing in her own home. When we first spoke on the phone, Natasha broke down in tears talking about how she was desperate to avoid giving her daughter the same upbringing she'd had, but she felt angry at her daughter's lack of respect, which triggered further arguments and subsequent guilt. Natasha also felt like a failure, despite working tirelessly to get through her workload, keep the house tidy, cook the meals and take care of life admin. She was exhausted and unsure what to do next.

We explored the Sky+ Box analogy together and then played out some of Natasha's thoughts, to see if they were high- or low-quality programming. She realised quickly the role semantics were playing in her present experience, demanding of herself, 'I *must* do everything *all* of the time' combined with, 'I'm *never* doing enough.' The natural result of these beliefs was an exhausting whirlwind of activity combined with a constant background sense of failure. In relation to her daughter, she held previously subconscious beliefs including, 'She's taking me for a *fool,*' and, 'She *should* listen to me because I'm her mother,' which naturally triggered feelings of anger and drove conflict.

Natasha played with softening her language, alongside forming new and helpful beliefs, such as, 'I aim to do my best both at work and home, while accepting I'm human and will therefore need downtime, too.' In relation to her daughter, she carved out beliefs such as, 'My daughter is learning and growing. I choose to have open and honest conversations with her when I feel her behaviour could be improved and will do everything I can to support her with this.'

In our next session, Natasha looked markedly more relaxed and at peace. Much of the conflict in her home had already dropped away, and a few months later she let me know her chronic sense of failure and guilt no longer played out. The damaging thought and behaviour patterns established in her own childhood were now consigned to the past.

Moving from rigid to flexible language

Take a few minutes to think about the *shoulds*, *musts* and *have-tos* that are playing out in different areas of your life. Have a play with rewording them to become more flexible, realistic and helpful:

- I should...   becomes   I could...
- I have to...   becomes   I choose to...
- I need to...   becomes   I intend to...

Which sentences do you prefer and which make you feel more motivated to take positive action? Add these to your Purpose Primer to help you internalise them.

Another area where semantics make a big difference is our tendency to use overly dramatic language. Consider the sentences below:

- This weather is shocking!

- It's raining.

- His behaviour was a disgrace!

- His behaviour wasn't ideal given the circumstances.

- This is the end of the world!

- This is a challenging situation.

- What a nightmare!

- This isn't the outcome I'd hoped for.

- I'm starving!

- I'm hungry.

These are just a few examples, but we could fill several pages here! Being neutral, our mind trusts what we say (our programming) without question, so the language we use can be the source of much of the stress and anxiety we experience. Your mind really does believe you when you say things are *shocking*, a *disgrace* and a *nightmare*, and will trigger a corresponding emotional reaction in your body. This is why many people suffering from severe anxiety experience the same panic and fear at work as one might expect in a war zone. Your mind trusts you when you tell it you're about to get *fired* and that this would be the *end of the world*, so it triggers your fight or flight response. But with no enemies to defeat or escape routes to run down, you have nowhere to channel this potentially toxic energy.

Semantics, then, are not just words: they are programming and, as with your beliefs, it's imperative that you choose wisely.

Reverse-engineer your life

In order to use your mind optimally, it's important to start with a clear picture of what you wish to achieve in any given situation (both in terms of your intended outcome and your desired internal state). You can then work backwards from that ideal, consciously selecting the programming that will take you there.

For example, imagine you're about to go on a first date. Without a clear picture of how you want the date to go or how you want to feel, you're leaving things up to chance and increasing the risk that the date won't go as you hope. If unwanted thoughts such as, 'First dates are scary,' or 'What if I can't think of anything to say?' arise, you may find yourself unwittingly triggering your fight or flight response, which is unlikely to play out well! How, then, might you consciously build a mindset to support you in this situation?

Your first question might be, 'What kind of date do I want this to be?' Let's imagine the answer comes back, *Fun, genuine and relaxed.* Now you're empowered to ask yourself, 'What true and helpful beliefs about myself and this situation will help make this date fun, genuine and relaxed?' This time the answer may come back, *First dates can feel a little nerve-wracking at first, but it's also exciting to meet someone new,* or, *I'm genuinely fascinated to find out more about their life and look forward to getting to know them better.* You may also choose to visualise yourself feeling relaxed, laughing and having fun in your mind's eye, to help crystallise the state you're aiming for.

By picturing the kind of date you want to experience, you're able to consciously choose the mindset that makes this possible. This is, of course, not to say you're in control of everything, but you give yourself the best possible chance for success in all situations when you begin with the end in mind.

Go beyond affirmations

Many personal development books advocate the use of affirmations, but there are conflicting accounts of what they are and how they need to be applied, in order to be effective. Tying in with our understanding of the mind, the most important realisation is that affirmations don't work if you're trying to *trick* yourself into believing something you know to be untrue. This is because it's not possible – or even desirable – to trick your mind, as it has instant access to everything you consciously and subconsciously know to be true. Therefore, if you were to repeat the affirmation, 'I am strong and powerful' while deep down believing you're weak, this would have little impact other than making you feel insincere.

While there are some potential challenges with the use of affirmations, this isn't to dismiss the concept altogether. When you're affirming something you already know deep down to be true, you remind yourself of – and step into – your full potential. In this way, rather than being *affirmations*, these are more *priming statements* that prepare you for optimal performance. The most powerful statements here are *I Am* statements. We spoke earlier about – often unconscious – *I Am* beliefs that can be self-limiting, such as 'I am weak'. To show up fully in the world, you'll want to instead have a set of consciously chosen *I Am* statements that are both true and helpful.

How I prime my mind

Over the years, I've found that it serves me — and, more importantly, my clients — if I prepare for a coaching session by reading a short list of priming statements. For example, 'I am an exceptional listener, listening through my mind, heart and gut,' primes me to fully tune into my client and listen beyond the words. 'I understand all insight occurs in the client' and 'I hold the silence and stillness in which shifts occur,' remind me to bite my tongue when I'm tempted to fill the silence unnecessarily within a session.

I'm careful to make sure that each of my priming statements is one hundred per cent true and helpful so that, rather than being false affirmations, they simply enable me to show up precisely as my client needs me to. This is not an ego-boosting exercise, as my only goal is to step into a selfless state, where I can serve my client powerfully in the moment.

I also have a list of *I Am* statements that I read as part of my morning preparation, alongside reviewing my vision, purpose and values. Statements such as, 'I am exactly where I'm meant to be at this moment' and 'I am open to the perfect lessons life is giving me,' help to keep me humble, present and open to growth opportunities. I'm priming myself to remember what I know to be important, but may otherwise forget in the busyness of everyday life.

Two of the most successful coaches in the world — Tony Robbins and Marshall Goldsmith — both speak about the ↲

importance of their daily rituals, to help ensure they consciously step into their optimal state. We have each learned through experience that, left to chance, we may not show up as we desire, and it's therefore vital that we set up a system to ensure our clients always experience transformational sessions.

So, why are *I Am* statements so powerful? Let's take the example: 'I am fully mindful of whatever is unfolding here and now.' By saying this statement, it's as if you're stepping into this truth. It's present tense, so you experience its effect instantly. The difference between this and saying, 'I will try to be mindful of whatever is unfolding here and now' is like night and day. To 'try' implies the action is not fully under your control. For example, try to pick up a pen now. If you picked it up, then you didn't *try* to do it, you did it. We are either mindful or we aren't. In addition, 'I will try to be mindful' also implies mindfulness is a future state, but as we know, mindfulness is now or never. Once again, simple semantics have a profound impact on the results we achieve, and *I Am* statements are as powerful as they come.

Before you begin to shape your own *I Am* statements, it's important to clarify once more that, while they can – for maximum impact – end up being powerfully worded, using them as a way to trick your mind about your current capabilities won't serve you. For example, after years of honing your craft, you may end up affirming, 'I am an exceptional public speaker' before you step on stage and this will serve you (and your audience) powerfully when it's both true and helpful.

However, shortcutting to this priming statement when you're at the start of your speaking journey will feel inauthentic, and therefore won't have the desired impact. Instead, a series of progressive primers, starting with something like, 'I am beginning the journey to becoming an exceptional speaker and am open to feedback,' will free you up to accelerate your development to the point where more powerful primers become true and helpful, and can therefore be adopted. Similarly, primers such as, 'I am perfect, whole and complete' have the potential to be very powerful, but only when you genuinely believe they are true – something we'll come onto when we explore self-worth in our journey shortly. The key here is not to repeat a statement you believe to be untrue, in the hope it overrides old thought patterns, but rather to have the insight that allows you to see this as your genuine reality and then consciously reinforce it.

Crafting your *I Am* statements

Take a few minutes to draft five to ten *I Am* statements that will help you step into your best self and enable you to live fully *on purpose*. Then add them to your Purpose Primer.

Step into unshakeable confidence

Self-confidence is something we'd all love and it can be a huge asset in life. But confidence can seem an elusive concept and your attempts to capture it can sometimes feel like chasing shadows. So, why is this, and how do you build unshakeable confidence?

In her timeless book, *Feel The Fear And Do It Anyway*, Susan Jeffers articulated that our deepest shared fear is that if something goes wrong, we won't be able to handle it. Moving beyond this fear is the foundation on which unshakeable self-confidence is built.

Let's place this fear under the spotlight and see if it stands up to scrutiny: 'If something goes wrong, I won't be able to handle it.' Is this one hundred per cent true? Under examination, we realise the answer is *no*. Think now of one thing – *anything* – that you haven't been able to handle in your life until this moment (and to give you a clue, to be able to read that sentence you've already proven that you've been able to handle it, because you're still here). It doesn't matter how much you've suffered, how scared you've been or what the current circumstances of your life are: you've survived it all and learned countless lessons along the way. You've been able to handle *everything* life has thrown at you –

and all without an instruction manual for your mind.

Now let's examine whether this same belief is helpful: does it take you where you want to go? Once more, we see it doesn't. A belief that you won't be able to handle something going wrong will inevitably stop you from stepping out of your comfort zone or expanding your capabilities. This belief alone will prevent you from building genuine self-confidence and living *on purpose*. True, unshakeable confidence comes when you don't need everything in the world to work out perfectly for you to feel self-assured; you simply know deep down that whatever happens, you'll handle it.

Realising that you can handle anything

Add the belief, 'I can handle anything' to your Purpose Primer, if it's not already on there.

An important clarification here is that having confidence doesn't make you great at everything, nor will you necessarily enjoy whatever you turn your hand to. When we don't fully grasp this, it's easy to beat ourselves up when we struggle, undermine our own confidence and stay stuck as a result. For example, if you're struggling in your current job (because it happens to be out of alignment with your values, purpose, strengths and passions), it's natural that you'll feel unconfident (because it's not where you're meant to be). However, if you put this down to *your* failings, rather than the situation, you further undermine yourself. You may then feel your confidence is too low to risk making a change, and decide to stick where you are until you can 'get your confidence levels up.'

If the reason you're unhappy is simply that you're out of alignment, then this approach is doomed to failure. More time passes, your confidence drops further, you decide there's something wrong with *you* and put your dream career move on the backburner for good. Crucially, confidence is situation-specific and intimately tied to your values, purpose and element.

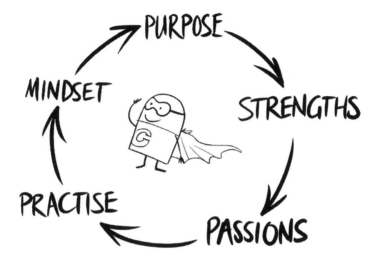

Built upon the foundation that you can handle *anything*, here are the five steps to creating unshakeable self-confidence:

Step one: make sure you are *on purpose*

If you're asked to do something *off* purpose you'll naturally struggle. It's when you align your life around your values and purpose that you'll experience a natural inner confidence, simply because you're being true to who you are and what you're here to do.

Step two: play to your strengths

If you're great at communicating with passion, you'll love the sales floor; if you're a natural cook, you'll feel confident in the kitchen. There's simplicity in aligning your life around your strengths. You can still work on building your expertise in areas beyond your core skillset, but confidence is a natural by-product of knowing you're good at something, so use that to your advantage.

Step three: follow your passions

You could be great at numbers, but the thought of working for an accountancy firm may leave you cold if your true passion is helping others to develop. Teaching maths may be the place where you'll thrive, and therefore where your confidence will naturally spike. Remember, your element – where your passions and strengths combine – is where your confidence will be at its highest.

Step four: practise

Your confidence will naturally increase when you take your skills to the next level, through repetition, practise and mental rehearsal. We'll explore how to accelerate this process on the next stage of our journey.

Step five: build a confidence mindset

Once you're playing in the right space and have honed your skills, it's your mindset that allows you to step into unshakeable self-confidence. To build a confidence mindset, it's important that you first become conscious of what might hold you back. Ask yourself, 'What do I currently believe about myself or this situation that will stop me from excelling?' Then consider whether these beliefs are one hundred per cent true and helpful, and rework them until they are. Next ask, 'What could I believe about myself and this situation that would free me up to excel?' In the same way that a skilled tailor ensures a finished suit perfectly fits the lines and contours of their client's body, imagine you're carving out a mindset perfectly tailored to the situation at hand.

Building unshakeable confidence

Bring to mind an area of your life where you'd like to develop more self-confidence, in order to live *on purpose*. Review each of the five steps above and consider what changes you could make at each stage to increase your confidence. After completing the final step, add your newly formed confidence mindset to your Purpose Primer.

Know your inherent self-worth

A strong and enduring sense of self-worth is a key component of living *on purpose* and yet, as with confidence, it can often be fleeting or elusive. So why does our sense of worth fluctuate, and what can we do to move beyond this experience? Crucially, we need to distinguish between our perceived and inherent self-worth.

At present, the majority of us search for ways to measure our *perceived* self-worth, deriving it from three sources. First, we look for it in our successes or failures; second, in the judgements of others; and finally, in our own self-judgements. However, by unwittingly tethering our self-worth to factors that aren't fully within our control, our self-worth naturally fluctuates.

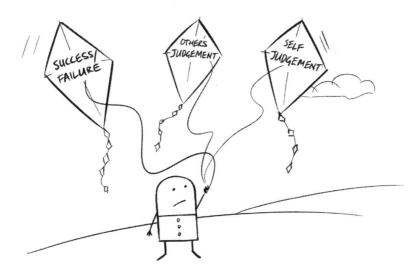

For example, if you base your self-worth on your successes and failures in the world, then even something beyond your control, such as an economic crisis, might have a detrimental impact on your perceived worth. Despite giving your best as a valued longstanding employee, your company might fold, meaning you're forced out of work. Or a financial investment you've made might suddenly prove worthless. If you've tethered your worth to your successes and failures, then it too will suffer, even though you played no part in this outcome.

You run into similar challenges if you're looking for your self-worth in the judgements of others. Imagine working for an insecure boss who feels threatened by conscientious employees. When you receive an unfair negative performance appraisal, your perception of your worth will drop if you believe it's influenced by their judgement. Once more, this isn't *self*-worth, as it has nothing to do with *you*. We also often find that the judgements we perceive others to be making are actually *our own* fears projected onto them. Have you ever wrongly assumed someone is making a negative judgement about you, only to discover they've been wrapped up in their own issues? We typically don't get to find out what someone *actually* thinks of us.

The final place we typically search for our worth is in our own self-judgements – what we think and believe about ourselves. Surely *this*, you may argue, is the source of true self-worth? However, when we look closely, this isn't fully within your control either. A typical person has somewhere in the region of twelve thousand to sixty thousand thoughts each day, and approximately eighty per cent of these thoughts tend to be negative.[12] Are you conscious of each of these thoughts? Are they all true and helpful? Unlikely! Some of them will be positive self-referencing ones, while others will be negative. Some days you'll look in the mirror and think you look great and some days you won't. Some days you'll think you're a good person and some days you won't. Therefore, tethering your self-worth to your own fleeting self-judgement is another risky option.

It's therefore crucial that we move beyond our current understanding of self-worth, which is based upon fluctuating circumstances and perceptions, to something that actually serves us.

---

12 Figures from the National Science Foundation.

Moving from perceived to inherent self-worth

In actual fact, you have an *inherent* value and worth, regardless of your outcomes in the world, other people's opinions of you or your own transitory thoughts. Put simply: *your self-worth isn't up for grabs.*

To help illustrate what inherent self-worth looks like, consider a baby boy: newborn and perfect. Let's give this child a value of one hundred out of a possible one hundred – a rating most of us would agree with. What happens when he becomes a toddler and is learning to walk? He keeps falling over and making mistakes. Compared with us, his ability as a walker is pretty poor! However, what's his value? It remains at one hundred. He's exactly where he's meant to be in his development at this moment in time, considering the motor skills at his disposal. Now imagine this same child a couple of years later, this time learning to read and write, and making hundreds of mistakes a day. His value remains at one hundred; this is a natural part of the learning process. Let's fast-forward. Imagine this child, now a young man at university, making some mistakes in his first-year exams that leads to an expected 2:2 rather than the 2:1 he'd been aiming for: value one hundred. He learns from this experience, takes the next paper and aces it with a first: value one hundred. A few years later, he gets married to his university sweetheart: value one hundred. He loses a job: value one hundred. He starts his own business: value one hundred. The business struggles in its first three years: value one hundred. His marriage breaks up: value one hundred. The business brings in its first six-figure year: value one hundred. He remarries: value one hundred. And so on.

Just as the toddler was perfect despite his 'imperfections', you too are perfect, despite your own current *perceived* 'imperfections'. Having imperfections is part of being human – it's what drives us to the next stage in our personal evolution. But you lose none of your innate perfection through this process. This paradigm shift is where true self-worth lies. The intriguing paradox is that, by recognising your underlying perfection, you're then freed up to work on your surface level 'imperfections' in a way that wasn't previously possible. You're no longer expending energy trying to protect your vulnerable ego or hide your weaknesses, and are instead open to areas of stretch and challenge that fast-track your skill development. In a way, you return to the perfect learning state that was your default as a toddler, now also armed with the full mental capacities that come with adulthood.

Now let's see what happens to self-worth when other people's judgements enter the fray. Let's rewind to when the boy was first learning to read. Imagine that his mother – due to her own challenging past and subsequent low self-worth – is an excessively judgemental parent. Imagine she grows frustrated by his inability to read sentences as quickly as other children in his class. She brands him *slow* and, as such, *her* perception of his worth drops from one hundred to seventy. Has *his* worth actually dropped as a result? Of course not. And this holds true throughout his lifetime, no matter who might be doing the judging. If a university lecturer lowers his estimation of the young man after judging his 2:2 in the first year to be a failure, once more this doesn't affect his inherent worth. It's simply a judgement – or a belief – and as we have seen, many of the beliefs we hold aren't true or helpful.

Even if this boy – influenced by the negative judgements of others – comes to *perceive* his own self-worth as having dropped, it still hasn't. So even if he believes his mum's criticism and thinks he's slow, this is just a belief. Even the judgements you make about yourself cannot, in reality, affect your self-worth, for your worth is *untouchable*. It's only your *perceived* self-worth that can ever fluctuate, and perceiving your own worth as low will never serve you. There may well be work to do on untrue and unhelpful beliefs formed, in part, from others' judgements, but as soon as that's done, the innate self-worth (which never went anywhere anyway) will be uncovered once more.

This new understanding of self-worth can help us move beyond perfectionism, which often arises from a deep-seated fear that we're imperfect. By understanding the paradox that you can be perfect at your core while still making mistakes in the world, you move beyond any need to hide or cover up your 'imperfections'. It also moves you beyond fear of failure, as winning or losing suddenly doesn't matter so much. You can still have a strong intent to win, but are freed up by knowing your worth doesn't depend upon the outcome.

Regardless of your past mistakes and failures, what others may have said about you, or your own negative self-judgments, you are – and always have been – perfect. Nothing from your past has diminished your worth in any way and nothing that lies ahead can do so, either. You are perfectly imperfect, and precisely where you're meant to be at this stage of your journey.

Realising your inherent self-worth

Add a belief related to this paradox – such as, 'I am perfect and still have a lot to learn' – to your Purpose Primer.

Client case study – Julie

We drew upon Julie's story earlier, but the shift she experienced after our work on self-worth was so profound, I thought it worth revisiting briefly here. For her whole adult life, Julie had assumed her worth had been destroyed by her early experiences of sexual abuse: she viewed herself as 'damaged goods' and suffered through periods of deep shame. However, after exploring the model of inherent self-worth, Julie experienced a sudden shift and an enormous resulting sense of freedom. After our work together, she felt compelled to email: 'I can honestly say I get it now. I almost feel like a different person – I am totally comfortable and happy with who I am and have a sense of inner peace. Life actually seems easy!' She understood for the first time that, while she'd had a terrifying period in her past, her value as a person had in no way been diminished: she was finally free from the binds of her childhood.

Balancing power and humility

Living *on purpose* compels us to step into our full potential, so we can add maximum value to the world in the time given to us. Therefore, when building your mindset, it's important to understand there's nothing admirable about limiting yourself or hiding your capabilities. As Nelson Mandela wisely stated, 'There is no passion to be found playing small – in settling for a life that is less than the one you are capable of living.'

Meekness is often confused with humility. But meekness – being submissive – is fundamentally different to humility. Humility simply means to not view yourself as more important or worthy than others.

Unlike meekness, this has nothing to do with not fulfilling your own potential. It's perfectly possible to become the best in your field while remaining humble. In fact, this delicate balance has been struck by all our great role models.

As we now understand through our new model of self-worth, our achievements don't elevate us above others, for our worth is always equal. We know that, in time, others will come to surpass our accomplishments through the fulfilment of their own purpose, and this no longer holds any threat to our self-esteem. Indeed, we understand that by stepping into our own potential, we inspire others to step into theirs, so our achievements light the way for even greater accomplishments.

Stepping into your power with humility

Add a related belief – such as, 'I am powerful and humble' – to your Purpose Primer.

Bringing it all together

The mindset you adopt is crucial to the impact you can have in the world. Until now, you may have looked on enviously at top performers, wishing you'd been bestowed with the innate self-confidence, worth, or ability to perform under pressure they appear to have been gifted with. But now you know differently. Every top performer in their field adopts a mindset that sets them up for success, and you now have everything you need to create and tailor your own. This is not about imitating others' approach or coveting their achievements, but rather finding your own authentic self and stepping into it fully. This is where your true power lies.

With a comprehensive understanding of mindset in place, you'll now be able to accelerate your skills development, taking your performance and impact to a new level. This is where we'll head next.

Reflection

- Where are you currently playing small in your life and what's the cost of doing so?
- Who is the top performer within your chosen field and what mindset do you think they've carved out to make their achievements possible?
- What's your key insight from this stage of our journey and what will you do differently as a result?

STAGE SIX

PREPARING FOR YOUR PUSH
TO THE SUMMIT

Skillset – what is your true potential?

'There is nothing noble in being superior to your fellow man; true nobility is being superior to your former self.'
Ernest Hemingway

'I have been impressed with the urgency of doing. Knowing is not enough; we must apply. Being willing is not enough; we must do.'
Leonardo da Vinci

The closer you get to your goal, the more challenging the terrain will become. You may face obstacles that, no matter your mindset, you simply can't overcome with your current skillset. If you were scaling a mountain, it would be the equivalent of reaching a sheer rock face without having trained to that grade of difficulty. You know it's possible to overcome these obstacles because others have done so before you, but there's no shortcut. You need to upskill and enhance your current capabilities as quickly as possible in order to continue your ascent. This stage of our journey is about mastery.

Which skills do you want to develop?

The work you began on adopting a growth mindset in the last stage of our journey lays the foundation for developing your skillset. The belief that you're capable of more than you're currently demonstrating, combined with a dedication to your own development, opens the door. Now you need to step through it and put in place concrete steps that lead to the achievement of your full potential. Knowing you can improve in all areas of your life, but that you have a finite amount of time to play with, the first step is to decide which skills you choose to develop. To do so, let's use one of the simplest yet most effective tools in coaching: the coaching wheel.

Creating a skills wheel

When you're ready, find a spare hour in your diary to create a skills wheel. You can use the one below, or download a printable version at *stevechamberlain.co.uk/livingonpurpose*.

You'll see there are eight segments, which typically works

well as a starting point. However, there are no hard and fast rules here, so if you find yourself identifying fewer skills you want to work on, that's perfectly fine, as is identifying more than eight (just create your own additional segments). This is all about what works for you.

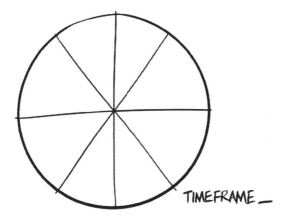

TIMEFRAME __

Step one: identify the skills you want to develop

The first thing to do is identify the skills you wish to hone. We're moving beyond the realm of *shoulds* here, so there's no external standard or expectation you need to live up to when making your choices. For example, if you feel you *should* work on your sales skills, but this doesn't tie in with your purpose, feel free to leave this out of your wheel. What you're looking for is a set of skills that excite you: things you'd love to be exceptional at, but where you currently feel there's room for improvement. Revisiting your values and purpose, then, is the key to finding the most important skills for inclusion. Try asking yourself the following question and see which answers arise for you:

'Knowing my core values are [insert core values] and that my purpose is [insert purpose], which skills, if developed, will enable me to have the maximum positive impact in the world?' ↩

Add the skills you identify through this process into the segments on your coaching wheel. The type of skills you might include range all the way from soft skills, such as *listening* or *building empathy*, to practical skills, such as *public speaking* or *delegation*, to technical skills, such as *illustration* or *coding*. As with your values, there are no right or *wrong* choices here, and your wheel will be unique to you. It may take a few minutes to decide which skills you choose to develop, but you'll know you've chosen wisely if the final wheel excites you. As a final test, before moving on to step two, answer the following questions:

- *'If I become highly proficient in each of these areas, will I have accelerated the fulfilment of my purpose?'*

- *'Are there any skills that will be more important than those currently included, that I choose to swap in?'*

Step two: establish your baseline

Now you have the skills you wish to work on, the next step is to identify your current level of proficiency in each of these areas. To do so, we'll use a simple scale of zero to ten, with zero indicating you currently have no proficiency in this area, ten indicating you're fully proficient, and five being the midway point. Again, this process is personal to you, so one person's four may be another person's seven.

Beginning with whichever segment you choose, ask where you'd currently score yourself in this area, from zero to ten. Once you have a number that feels like a fair reflection, mark this with a line across the segment at the appropriate point (for example, if you were giving a score of five, you'd draw a line through the midway point of the segment) and write the number beside this line, so you can easily see your current score at a glance. Continue this process until each segment has a line and an associated number: this represents your baseline.

Step three: establish your goal

The next step is to decide your ideal score for each of your skills, within a given timeframe. To do this, begin by choosing a date you'd like to see an improvement by. This could be a few months from today, a year, or further into the future. Again, there's no right or wrong here, so consider what would be a motivating and achievable target date for you to work towards.

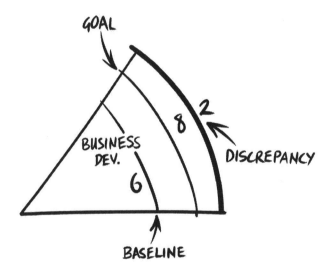

Once you have your timeframe, revisit each segment in your wheel and decide what score you'd like to have achieved by that point in time. For example, you may have decided your business development skills are currently a six and that, one year from now, you want to increase this to eight. Once again, there are no hard and fast rules. Some people will have big discrepancies between their baseline and target scores, while others will have smaller differences. You may also have some areas where you feel it's not realistic or important to ↩

improve within your target timeframe. You might choose to revisit these after you have achieved progress with your higher-priority skills.

When you know your target score, draw a separate line across each segment to represent where you wish to get to within your chosen timeframe. Write this target number beside the new line, so you can again see your scores at a glance. When you're finished, you'll have two lines for each segment of your wheel, one showing your current baseline and another showing your target. Write the discrepancy between your current and target score for each of the segments. For example, in the above business development example, the difference between the current score of six and target proficiency of eight is two. By doing this for each of the segments, you'll have a snapshot of your 'gap to goal' for each skill.

Step four: determine your priority areas

Now you're ready to establish which will be your priority area(s) to focus on first. Trying to focus on all eight skills simultaneously will leave you stretched too thin and unable to achieve any tangible results, which can prove demotivating. Deciding which skills you want to target first is an important step in building confidence and achieving mastery.

Some people find that prioritising areas with the biggest discrepancy scores works well. Others prefer to go with their gut instinct on which skills feel most important right now. Whichever approach appeals, begin by identifying your top three priority skills. This doesn't mean the other skills aren't important and, in time, you'll focus on all of them. But it does allow you to home in on particular priority areas for now. Once you have your top three, you're ready for the final step.

Step five: create an action plan

Now you have your target list, the final step is to put practical steps in place that will take you from your current to desired level of proficiency within your chosen timeframe. To do so, you'll want to establish some clear criteria that define what reaching your target score would look like in reality. The following questions will help guide this process:

- By [insert target date], what would my proficiency in this area need to look like to have achieved my target rating of [insert target rating]? What will I be thinking, feeling and doing?

- What concrete actions will enable me to take my proficiency to the target level?

- Which resources can I draw upon, and who do I know who could help accelerate my development in this area?

Setting SMART goals as part of this step will again help to ensure your goals are Specific, Measurable, Attainable, Relevant and Time-bound. The clearer you can be on what success looks like, the more likely it is you'll achieve your aim. For example, the target of achieving a score of eight out of ten for business development could be measured by accomplishing concrete goals, such as attending a training course, creating a two-page strategy document and making at least six new business approaches, all by your set date.

Now you have your skills wheel laid out and your first goals set, it's important that you regularly revisit this tool in order to track your progress and set new priorities over time. If, by your target date, business development has indeed improved from a six to an eight, it's up to you whether you move the goalposts once more, to take this skill to a nine or a ten, ↵

or choose to switch your focus to your next priority area(s). Once you've achieved your objective in all areas, your current wheel will have served its purpose and you'll likely feel compelled to create a new one, capturing additional skills that are now required as your impact grows. Mastery is a lifelong process and, ultimately, there's always more you could choose to learn and develop.

Client case study – James

James was the founder and CEO of one of the UK's leading marketing agencies. We began coaching during a period of rapid expansion for his business, where his workload had increased significantly, triggering chronic anxiety, as well as periods of acute stress and associated health problems. Two weeks before working together, he had experienced his first panic attack, which led him to seek help.

James's long-term goal was to be able to step back from the day-to-day running of the business, so he could stop working twelve-hour days and spend more time with his family (his number-one core value). We began by identifying and reworking the underlying beliefs that were driving his stress and explored how he could apply mindfulness to bring a calm focus to his work. Within a couple of weeks, his stress had subsided, and he was now ready to focus on his overarching goal.

Within four years, James wanted his business to be able to run just as smoothly without him in the office as when he was present, enabling him to achieve his ambition of taking his family to the Florida Keys for three months. In the meantime, he wanted to be able to leave the office no later than 6pm; to work one day a week from home; and start taking more short breaks with his family. Using the coaching wheel, James mapped out what would need to come together for him to realise these goals.

The segments he identified were *organisation*, *delegation*, *trust*, *culture*, *delivery*, *work ethic*, *leadership*, *recruitment and retention*, *communication* and *wellbeing*. He set current baseline and target scores for each, and then homed in on his first priority area: *recruitment and retention*. The steps he identified to take him to his target score included: creating a range of new roles, including a project manager to handle the company's workstream; advertising these roles within three months; building a pool of ten freelancers for different areas of the business within six months; resolving a disciplinary issue with a current employee; and providing additional training for a promising member of the team. He diarised and delegated each of these areas that day.

Just a month later, James had achieved his goal of working from home one day a week. He was also dropping his son off at school before swimming on another and finished early on Fridays. He subsequently enjoyed a three-week family holiday in Asia and, with the new processes in place, returned to a well-oiled business. The Florida Keys are now well within his sights.

Ineffective versus effective skill development

'Ever since I was a child, I have had this instinctive urge for expansion and growth. To me, the function and duty of a quality human being is the sincere and honest development of one's potential.'

Bruce Lee

Knowing the skills you wish to work on, along with your desired outcome and target date, gives you the perfect platform on which to build your skillset. But this isn't the whole picture. Your success in achieving your goals and the pace at which you develop will, ultimately, come down to how you apply yourself. An ineffective approach to skill development can leave you scratching your head as to why you haven't achieved the desired results when your deadline arrives. This, in turn, can lead to a sense of powerlessness and a resulting drop in motivation. Mastery in skill development, on the other hand, will see you achieving and even surpassing your stated targets, leading to a sense of empowerment. How, then, do you step into the second space and set yourself up for success?

The key to continuous development is becoming conscious of precisely *why* your approach is or isn't working, and to then course correct as appropriate. No stone should be unturned and nothing left to chance in your pursuit of excellence. You'll seek out constructive (and sometimes challenging) feedback following your successes and setbacks, and will be willing to face your areas of weakness directly. This is about bringing your development from the unconscious realm into your conscious awareness.

Let's explore six factors that influence the speed at which you'll attain mastery in your chosen field.

1. Questions to accelerate your development

High-quality questions enable you to bring into your conscious awareness both the beliefs and behaviours that may be holding you back, as well as those that are aiding your development. The following coaching questions will greatly accelerate your progress in your chosen area of focus:

- What's stopping me from achieving my goal in this area?

- Which beliefs do I currently hold that are blocking my development?

- Where am I letting myself off the hook?

- Where am I playing small?

- What advice would I give a friend if they were facing the same challenge?

- Which three things could I do that would make a positive difference here?

- What do I need to believe about myself to achieve this goal?

- What do I need to believe about this goal in order to achieve it?

- What am I afraid of?

- What would I do if I were fearless?

- How could this be fun?

- What mindset do I need to adopt, in order to achieve my desired outcome?

- Five years from now, having successfully accomplished my goal, what have I done to get here and how did I do it?

- What am I currently doing that is working well?

- What could I do even better?

- What have I learned from this experience and what will I do differently as a result?

- Who do I know who excels in this area, and what mindset and approach do they adopt?

- If I knew my worth wasn't dependent upon the outcome, how might this free me up?

These questions shine a spotlight on what's inhibiting your progress, which then empowers you to make the appropriate changes. It isn't about self-criticism or judgement, but rather a balanced and considered appraisal of what's working and what isn't.

2. Practise, practise, practise

Once your values, purpose, beliefs, mindset and skillset are in alignment, there's only one thing for it. Get out there and practise. If you want to become an exceptional public speaker, take up every available opportunity to speak in front of an audience. After each engagement, use questions like the ones above to evaluate your performance and identify areas for improvement. Then put this to the test by going back into the arena again. It's on you to put yourself out there, learn your craft and give your all in every given moment. Only then will you see your full potential come to fruition.

3. Visualise success

Mentally rehearsing a desired outcome, such as delivering a great speech, is a powerful way to set yourself up for success. Ultimately, your mind doesn't know the difference between visualisation and reality, so you can programme yourself to be in the optimal state and experience the associated positive emotions ahead of the event. Then, when the moment arrives, you have a groove you can slip into; it's as if you've already been there, having performed with focus and composure.

Play with this tool by closing your eyes and visualising everything going exactly to plan. See the space, hear the sounds, and feel the associated positive emotions in your body and the elation as you achieve your goal.

4. Seek feedback

External feedback can be of huge value. Others see things we can't see ourselves, and we *all* have blind spots. Therefore, it can be invaluable to seek feedback and listen carefully for any insights you can apply going forwards. However, there's an important distinction to make here between constructive and unconstructive feedback. Constructive feedback is balanced, considered and helpful. Unconstructive feedback can actually be detrimental. For example, would it be a good idea for Roger Federer to ask *you* for advice on his tennis swing? Probably not. Similarly, some friends or family members may not be best positioned to deliver feedback, so choose your sources wisely. It's also a good idea to let people know in advance what you want them to look out for, to help ensure the data you receive really serves you.

5. Find a mentor

One of the most effective ways to fast-track your development is to find someone who already excels in your chosen area and ask them what they do. You may be surprised how flattered people are when you ask them for advice and, therefore, how open they are to sharing their experiences. Begin by considering who excels in your chosen field and then how you might be able to approach them. Being introduced by a friend or colleague often gives the best chance of success, as can making connections on platforms such as LinkedIn. A mentor can fast-track your development, as you get to learn from their successes and failures before walking the path yourself. Not all the advice will be relevant, but often there will be insights or lessons that save you considerable time or energy on your own journey.

If you're unable to find a suitable mentor, consider instead what beliefs someone at the top of their game in your field would need to hold, and what your role models do that works well. Reading autobiographies or watching interviews with these figures can be invaluable as part of this process. You're not trying to imitate, but rather to gain valuable information that you can then assimilate.

6. Get a coach

'Everyone needs a coach.'
Bill Gates, Microsoft co-founder

It's no coincidence that the world's most successful businesspeople, actors and sports stars all have coaches. They understand that remaining at the top of their field – and scaling even greater heights – is aided by working with a highly skilled coach, who can reveal their blind spots and unlock further potential.

There are some exceptional coaches out there and many different coaching styles. Therefore, it's important you get a good sense of any prospective coach's expertise and style, check out their client testimonials and success stories, and trust your gut instinct before committing.

Bringing it all together

You experience your peak states when achieving mastery in your chosen field. By developing your skills in alignment with your values and purpose, a true sense of fulfilment comes into your life. You're capable of more than you have ever believed possible: now it's up to *you* to make that your reality.

But you don't need to wait until you excel in your field, or achieve the trappings of success, before you can find happiness. The final stage of our journey takes us to the realisation of what we're all ultimately seeking: inner peace and contentment.

Reflection

- If you improved your priority skills by just five per cent each year, what difference would that make to your impact over the next decade?
- How could you fast-track your skill development over the next twelve months?
- What's your key insight from this stage of our journey, and what will you do differently as a result?

STAGE SEVEN

REACHING THE SUMMIT

Enlightenment – where does everything you seek lie?

'Is there a difference between happiness and inner peace? Yes. Happiness depends on conditions being perceived as positive; inner peace does not.'
Eckhart Tolle

'The universe is not outside of you. Look inside yourself; everything that you want, you already are.'
Rumi

Congratulations! You've arrived at the summit – the culmination of every conscious step taken in alignment with your values and in pursuit of your purpose. However, there's something you need to be aware of, if your journey isn't to be in vain.

The maximum recommended time for a mountaineer to remain in the 'death zone' at the summit of one of the highest peaks on Earth is just 15 minutes. Any longer and oxygen supplies diminish to a critical level. Following the necessity of a swift descent, over the following weeks this mountaineer is then likely to feel the inevitable low that follows the accomplishment of a lifetime goal. They may struggle to regain the state of fulfilment or contentment experienced so vividly at the summit and their motivation may flatline.

So it is for many of us: once we reach our intended destination in life, we find the happiness or bliss to be short-lived and our sense of fulfilment passing all too quickly. We can easily develop an insatiable thirst for *more* and lose sight of what led us to experience our peak states in the first place.

So, what *are* we ultimately searching for on our journey?

Inner peace and contentment – the pinnacle

You may, understandably, have expected happiness or bliss to be the culmination of your journey. Surely these are the states after which we strive the most, and therefore the rewards we should be reaping through a life lived *on purpose*? But while happiness and bliss are indeed peak states, they can't be the true pinnacle, for they aren't enduring or permanent. They are transient states and therefore not the ultimate destination. No matter how exhilarating they may feel, we know we will inevitably descend to lower ground before our next ascent, leaving a void that can be hard to reconcile.

While a life led *on purpose* will absolutely be defined by states of joy, happiness and bliss, enduring inner peace and contentment is the ultimate human accomplishment. They are the constants that can become the background to all our experiences, including our peak states. Crucially, they can also endure through our most challenging times, too – our descents – which is why we come to them for the final stage of our journey. Let's explore what true inner peace looks like, why it's so important and how you can cultivate it.

A key distinction – happiness versus contentment

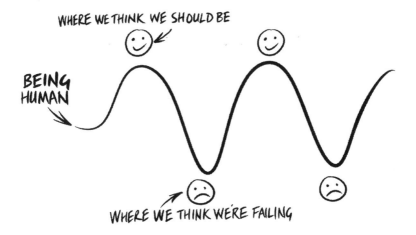

Happiness is a feeling or emotion, and is therefore a transient state that can come and go. Contentment and inner peace, on the other hand, can be experienced as a permanent background state within which other emotions (both positive and negative) can be experienced. Happiness exists in the world of poles – good vs bad; rich vs poor; healthy vs unhealthy; happy vs unhappy. In the same way that you cannot flip heads on a coin without the possibility of also flipping tails, it's impossible to feel happiness without also sometimes experiencing its opposite, unhappiness. If you're currently feeling happy, when you look closely you realise that you're certain to experience unhappiness at some future point. The happiness of going on holiday is followed by the come down upon your return. The happiness of being with your extended family for Christmas is followed by the inevitable sadness of leaving (depending on your relations, of course!). On a smaller scale, the happiness of purchasing new clothes is followed by the sadness of seeing them fade or get damaged over time. This is not to be pessimistic, but simply to observe one of the principles of our universe. What, then, is the alternative?

Contentment (perpetual inner peace) exists beyond poles. It's a feeling that life is fine just as it is, and that it will still be OK when your current experience passes. The word *contentment* in this context has no opposite: no flip side to the coin. It is the background sense of acceptance and trust, both in yourself and the process of life itself. It comes from aligning yourself with the present moment through the practice of mindfulness. You trust that everything is unfolding exactly as it needs to, and you trust in your ability to be able to handle both the ups and downs, without identifying with either. You allow yourself to fully experience your emotions, from joy and happiness through to sadness and grief. You accept reality and align yourself with life.

The power of non-attachment

'The root of suffering is attachment.'
Buddha

The secret to contentment is non-attachment. Non-attachment means to not identify with your thoughts, emotions, roles, successes, failures, or anything else on your journey. As we touched on earlier, *you* are the adventurer and the witness to whatever is unfolding, both within yourself and in the world as you explore. From this place, when you experience sadness, you relate to it in the same way you might relate to anything else you come across on your travels. You're aware of it, you sense it, you experience it, but in doing so you also come to know that it is not who *you* are. You also know this experience will pass, but that you won't be diminished in any way. Similarly, when you experience the highs of life and the positive emotions associated with this, you don't confuse these conditions or emotions with who you are. You experience them as you might enjoy a delicious meal, always understanding that this too will pass. When you sit as the witness in this way, you move beyond identification with the highs and lows of life, and are instead free to experience everything life has to offer, including the opportunity to play and create in the world. And you do so without fear. *This* is inner peace and it's available to all of us.

Our elusive search for happiness

'I think everybody should get rich and famous and do everything they ever dreamed of so they can see that it's not the answer.'
Jim Carrey

The reason your search for lasting happiness is on shaky ground is that you've likely been told to look for it in the wrong places and have therefore been striving for an unachievable goal. It's the equivalent of being sent on a quest to find the edge of the world before knowing it was round. Even the most skilled explorer would return disappointed. So it has been with our quest for happiness. There are four key places we've been told to search in vain…

1. Searching for enduring happiness in the future

The first place we've been led to believe enduring happiness lies is in the future. 'Once I'm older/when I no longer need to work/when X, Y or Z circumstance has changed, *then* I'll be happy.' However, as you know, your life unfolds in the now, always. The future never really arrives. If your former nows have been defined by a sense of waiting then, without an inner shift, your present will be experienced in the same way.

This is why many of us think happiness will come when we reach a future point, such as retirement, only to find it's still an elusive concept when we get there. So what do we typically do? We set it as another future goal: 'When I'm a couple of years into retirement and feeling settled in this new phase, I'll experience lasting happiness.' And so the search continues. Alternatively, we might reach retirement age and then reminisce to a time when we were younger and fitter, and wonder why we didn't enjoy our lives more then.

A personal reflection

Take a moment to consider whether you've ever thought that you'd be happy by this point in your life. How many times have you moved these goalposts within your lifetime? Do you still see lasting happiness as a future state?

2. Searching for enduring happiness through consumerism

Our consumer society is based upon the myth that *things* bring lasting contentment. The advertising world is made up of companies telling us we can buy happiness by owning or using their products. Drink this fizzy drink, and you too will look and feel like these beautiful, joyful people. The fact they all have pearly white teeth despite claiming the sugar-filled drink is a staple of their diet is not, in fact, the biggest lie here: it's the assertion that you will magically achieve contentment by buying their product.

The happiness that results from any purchase has a relatively short lifespan: the high from a soft drink is gone in a matter of minutes; the new mobile phone within a few weeks; even the new house within a year or so. Before long, inner dissatisfaction returns. So, what do we do? We make another, often bigger, purchase. We've been sold the illusion that once we have the dream car or house, we'll find lasting happiness. In time, this becomes a belief that drives our behaviour: our thirst for more becomes unquenchable.

To illustrate, let me share briefly the story of one of my coaching clients. He has a successful and lucrative career, a large house and a number of high-end cars, one of which represents the realisation of a childhood dream – a Ferrari. According to our Western society's current conception of happiness, this should have brought him endless joy and contentment. Not so. He *never* drives the Ferrari anymore; it sits in his garage, gathering dust. The reason: after the initial excitement a number of years back, driving it no longer makes him happy. He's bored of it. Which goes to show, even a childhood dream purchase will still leave you feeling empty in time. And if your dream purchase cannot make you happy then, quite simply, happiness cannot come from possessions.

3. Searching for enduring happiness through wealth

The next place we typically look for happiness is through wealth: 'If I won the lottery, I'd be happy for life.' When we hear stories of lottery winners who still don't seem happy, we find it incomprehensible. We think, 'If *I* won the lottery, I'd be ecstatic!' And you would, for a time. But this state of euphoria would pass. You may also start to experience doubts, such as, 'Are these new friends genuine, or are they only interested in my money?' You may feel like a fraud if you start hanging around in different, wealthier circles: 'What if they find out this was just a lottery win and I didn't earn it?' You may find you have little in common with your new crowd and that the money actually separates you from your old friends, who can't afford the same lifestyle, leaving you in a state of limbo.

Even if your money is self-made, we hear of millionaire businesswomen and men who still feel unhappy and fear they might lose it all. You'll probably also know people who have less money than you, but who seem more content and at peace. So of course, while a certain level of income (that enables us to afford the necessities of food, shelter and clothing) is crucial to contentment, enduring happiness doesn't lie in our financial wealth.

4. Searching for enduring happiness through status

Many of us believe that once we achieve that promotion, run our own business, get married or become a parent, we'll be happy. But once again, the happiness may be short-lived. The promotion comes with its own challenges; the business has its ups and downs; married life brings with it the daily challenges that come with sharing your life with another; and the joy of early parenting is counter-balanced by sleepless nights and seemingly *endless* loads of washing! *Every* role we play or status we achieve will change or come to pass in time. Therefore, looking to a certain role for enduring happiness isn't the answer, either.

The inner journey

'We shall not cease from exploration, and the end of all our exploring will be to arrive where we started and know the place for the first time.'

T.S. Eliot

These examples are not exhaustive, but give a flavour of the many places we often try to find lasting happiness. Our intent is positive and our goal admirable but, as with chasing shadows, we've set our sights on something that can't be captured. What is it, then, that ties all the above together? When we look closely, we realise they're all based on one core assumption – that happiness lies *outside* of us. We have believed (and have been told) that we need to find it – and then take it – to make us feel better. But what if happiness isn't a commodity to be bought or sold? What if it isn't something you can take from the world? What if it doesn't actually exist *out there*?

Inwards.

Where does contentment lie?

Bring to mind a time when you experienced profound happiness, joy, or contentment in your life. It might be a moment from a holiday, your early childhood, a relationship or work. When you have this moment in your mind's eye, consider the following questions:

- Did you experience this peak emotion of happiness, joy or contentment in the 'now' (at the precise moment it was happening)?
- Was the happiness, joy or contentment something you took from the situation, or was it something you experienced internally, as part of the unfolding experience?
- Now try to recall any time in your life when you've experienced happiness, joy or contentment outside of the present moment, or as something separate to you (not an internal state).

When you look closely, you will likely realise that the present moment is the *only* place you can ever experience happiness, joy or contentment. There has *never* been a time when you've experienced these states outside of the present moment and there never will be. You also realise that happiness, joy and contentment all lie within *you*. These states arise because you feel a deep sense of connection or oneness with life in any given moment. Sometimes this might come about when you're alone and still, on other occasions it may be when you're at one with nature, when you have a deep sense of connection with others, or through total immersion in the activity you're engaged with. Wherever and whenever you experience these peak states, you'll have done so by coming fully into the present moment.

Put simply, *everything* you're looking for is already within you and the very essence of who you are. You've likely been told to look outside of yourself for contentment and joy, which is why your search has been an impossible one. If your house keys were in your pocket, but you'd been told you'd dropped them outside, then your search could never be successful. So it has been in your search for lasting peace, love, joy and contentment. Like a grand illusion of Houdini proportions, where smoke and mirrors trick you into averting your gaze, your attention has been drawn into the world, rather than to the simplicity of the here and now, where you already have everything you seek.

With this realisation comes an enlightened life in which you're free to create, experience and evolve moment by moment. It's possible for *all* of us to achieve this state, as you're not attaining something that's not who you already are. In essence, you're simply returning to your true nature. Like a seeker who travels the world in search of contentment, only to return home to discover it was always there, so too are you now returning to your true self.

Contentment isn't in the fire

For my wife's thirty-fifth birthday, I bought her a fire pit. Not the most romantic of gestures, you might be thinking, but then you don't know my wife's values! *Freedom / wildness / adventure* is her combined fifth core value and, when put into the context of us both being tied to the house with two young children for the foreseeable future, it meant this wasn't such a bad present after all!

So it was that, aided by all the mod-cons, including a lighter and fire logs, we celebrated our first experience of building a fire (without any of the actual skill of our forefathers). We were proud nonetheless, and settled back to watch the flames grow as the sun set. We both felt a sense of true contentment: everything was exactly as it needed to be. This was a wise purchase indeed and meant – so I thought – we'd bought on-tap contentment, ready for us to access any time we chose.

A few weeks later, with the kids safely tucked up in bed, we lit a fire once more and I again eagerly anticipated the feeling of contentment I was certain would follow. I settled back and waited, but the state I achieved on the fire pit's first outing seemed frustratingly elusive. It wasn't that I had a *bad* evening, but I felt I'd missed something important as we headed indoors a few hours later.

Upon reflection, I'd made an association between building the fire and the peak state I'd experienced, and had assumed that getting the fire pit out again would automatically result in the same sense of peace. But my thinking was flawed. Contentment hadn't been caused by the fire pit; it had come about because I'd dropped all resistance to the present moment on that first night. On the second night, I was in a state of waiting. Contentment wasn't in the *fire;* it was in *me.* All I had to do was come back into the moment to connect with it once more.

The key realisation here is that we can't experience anything we *seek.* The very act of seeking something means we believe we don't already have it within us. And if we believe that to be true, then our experience will be one of lack, rather than one of contentment.

We often hear the term 'inner peace' or 'inner contentment', but never stop to consider the implication of these words. *Inner* peace; *inner* contentment. Not peace or contentment outside of yourself, but *within*, here and now. The beauty is you never have to go anywhere to experience it: what you seek is already within you.

Take a moment to check in with your heart or gut, to see whether this resonates with you. On some level, do you already know this to be true? If so, the implications for how you lead your life are profound.

But as enlightening as this sounds, you may understandably ask, if it's true that I have everything I seek within me, why don't I experience lasting contentment as my natural state? And how can I apply this knowledge practically in a challenging world?

The secret lies in aligning your life with your values.

And so we come full circle, back to where we began. Now you've followed each of the steps, this seemingly linear journey becomes a circuit, where you return to your core values in order to experience peace, love, joy and contentment through everything you do. Let's revisit your values now, to see how they can lead you back to the inner peace and contentment that's always been yours.

The values principle revisited

As we explored in the first stage of our journey, the values principle determines that you suffer when you're out of alignment with your core values, closing you off to your natural states of joy, inner peace and contentment. However, the moment you realign around your values, these peak states resurface. This is a principle that can be relied upon to play out *every* time, in much the same way that the law of gravity determines an apple will *always* fall to the ground. If you live your life out of alignment with your values, you *will* suffer, and the extent to which you're off track will determine the extent of your suffering. But the moment you realign, all suffering falls away and you experience the peace, love, joy and contentment after which you've been striving. Just as, with the flick of a light switch, a room goes from darkness to light without resistance or delay, so it is with your values.

The values principle explains why there's so much confusion about where happiness can be found. Everyone's values are unique, so happiness, joy and contentment will be found in different places for each of us. One person's joy is another person's suffering; one person's dream holiday is another's holiday from hell; one person's perfect job causes another chronic stress; one person's ideal partner drives another up the wall. Your values are unique, and it's only by understanding and aligning with them that you can lead a genuinely contented life.

We could compare the states of peace, love, joy and contentment to the sun on a cloudy day. Even though thick clouds may block the sun from your view, the moment they part, you experience its warmth instantly. In the same way, when your life is out of alignment with your values, you may feel a long way from inner peace and contentment, but the moment you realign, it's as if the clouds have parted and you experience them once more. The reality is, they never went anywhere. You simply lost your way temporarily.

We won't go into how to align your life with your values again here (revisit Chapter One for a reminder!). However, there's one further crucial distinction that needs to be understood, in order to experience lasting inner peace and contentment. To experience your peak states, you need to *give* to the world, not *take* from it.

To give is to receive

Our common understanding of giving and receiving tells us that if you give something away, you have less for yourself. For example, if you have five pound coins and give one away, you now have just four left. Through the act of giving, you've simultaneously lost something. It therefore makes sense for us to think of the energy we give to others in the same way. If you give love to someone else, you must have less love left to give – at least until your supplies can be replenished. But although this seems logical, experience tells us this isn't how things play out in reality. Imagine you shower your partner or children with love and affection all day. Rather than experiencing your supply of love as diminished, you too feel full of love – often more so than when the day began. This doesn't tally with our current understanding of giving, but holds true any time you live in alignment with your values: through the act of giving, you receive.

What about joy? Once again, we find we experience this peak state only when we align with our values and *give* to the world. For example, if three of your core values happen to be *love, charity* and *community*, then you'll naturally find yourself experiencing joy when supporting a local charity fun run, which aligns with each of these values. If, on the other hand, you value *leadership, accuracy* and *achievement,* you'll experience joy through expertly leading your team to deliver a challenging work project. The joy and contentment you experience in both examples isn't a result of receiving praise or recognition (unless these happen to be your values), but instead come through the act of *adding value* to the world.

The principle of giving to receive holds true irrespective of how much or little you perceive you have to give. Therefore, if you feel you're lacking in love, paradoxically this is a sign that you need to *give* love – to *be loving*. To give something you don't believe you possess is both a paradox and a leap of faith, but once taken, you come to realise you can *never* lack for anything again. If you want love, *be* loving; if you want joy, *be* joyous; if you want peace, *be* peaceful; if you want acceptance, *be* accepting and so on. This is true abundance.

You are already perfect (and have a lot to learn!)

The combination of these two key insights – that everything you're searching for is already within you; and what you give, you receive – leads to one core truth: you are *already* perfect, whole and complete. This understanding is enlightenment.

Of course, realising your innate perfection doesn't mean there's nothing for you to learn, nor does achieving inner peace and contentment mean you no longer aspire to new heights. Rather, these realisations free you up to lead a genuinely fulfilling life. You're free to try new things, make mistakes and push your boundaries, safe in the knowledge that, no matter the outcome, your inherent value is unaffected.

You may still choose to purchase designer clothes, fast cars or beautiful houses, but you no longer make the mistake of thinking you'll find something through those purchases that you don't already have. You still have romantic relationships, and build loving marriages and families, but now in the awareness that it's what you *give* to these relationships that will define them. You still set goals, seek job promotions and build success, but now in the knowledge that these experiences will only be fulfilling to the extent that they are aligned with your values and your purpose. The result is an enlightened life lived *on purpose,* where you return to your natural states of inner peace and contentment, and are freed up to add unique value to the world.

Bringing it all together

'In a gentle way, you can shake the world.'
Mahatma Gandhi

Imagine you're sat around an infinite canvas that stretches as far as the eye can see. Everyone you've ever met, or will ever meet, is there with you. On the canvas is painted everything that exists in your world. There are images of your community, car, house and all other possessions. You've spent your entire life here and, until this moment, have believed that, in order to experience happiness or to feel complete, you've needed to cut things out of this canvas to keep for yourself. So, you've taken your knife to the picture and cut out the car, the savings, the job role and so on. While this has been done with your best intentions – and this is what everyone sat next to you has been doing, too – it's never led to a feeling of contentment. Deep down, you sense that what you're doing isn't working. But it's all you've ever known and there doesn't seem to be another way, so you take out your knife once more and cut away something bigger from the canvas, in the hope this will be the one that changes everything.

Now consider someone you haven't met before sits down next to you. You sense in them a genuine contentment you haven't seen before so, intrigued, you watch what they do. The first thing you notice is they don't have a knife. Instead, they have a paint tray filled with vibrant colours and a brush. They lean over and begin to paint wonderful images onto the canvas. Before long, the space in front of them is alive with stunning colours. Then they get up and move to another place around the infinite canvas, to continue their creation.

You look down and notice for the first time that you, too, have paints and a paintbrush. Something inside you stirs, and you dip your brush into the paint to begin your own creation. For the first time in years, a genuine smile comes to your face and you begin to add to the mosaic. The person next to you looks up and watches what you're doing, with an expression of intrigue. After a few moments, you notice they too have found their paints and brush, and are leaning in to create.

You suddenly know the truth: that taking from the picture has never given you what you seek – and never will. For the first time, you realise you have your own unique pallet (your values) and the perfect paintbrush (your mind). You understand you're here to add to the infinite canvas (life), and that by doing so, you'll experience the joy of creation alongside all the love, inner peace and contentment you've ever sought.

And so, you paint.

Reflection

- Can you sense that everything you've ever strived for is inside of you, right now?
- Knowing that joy comes from *being* joyful, love comes from *being* loving and contentment comes from *being* contented, how do you choose to *be*?
- What is your key insight from the final stage of our journey, and what will you do differently as a result?

THE HIDDEN CHAPTER

During the editing process, a short chapter that fell between stages three and four was removed, to ensure there were no detours from the end destination. However, if you're in search of true transformation, it will still prove invaluable.

To receive this free hidden chapter and discover the insights, please spare a couple of minutes to review this book on Amazon or in a blog post, thereby helping others to live *on purpose*. I would love all reviews to be authentic and honest, so simply send a screenshot of whatever feels true to *hello@stevechamberlain.co.uk* and I'll send you the link.

THE ONWARD JOURNEY

Sharing your insights

I'd love to hear your questions, insights and success stories as you journey to living *on purpose*. Please share at *facebook.com/ stevechamberlaincoach* or join my community at *stevechamberlain. co.uk/livingonpurpose*.

Continuing the journey

If you're keen to continue your learning journey, **I highly recommend the following books**: *Mindset* by Carol Dweck, *The Element* by Sir Ken Robinson, *Somebody Should Have Told Us* by Jack Pransky, *The Power of Now* by Eckhart Tolle, *The Untethered Soul* by Michael A. Singer and *Extraordinary* by Elke Edwards.

If you're interested in exploring **one-to-one coaching**, I'd be delighted to connect – please visit *stevechamberlain.co.uk* to find out more, or email me at *hello@stevechamberlain.co.uk*.

If you work for, or lead, a company that's committed to creating more fulfilling workplaces and a more conscious world, you can find out about my **public speaking and live workshops** online at *stevechamberlain.co.uk/onpurpose*.

I'm also currently developing an **online programme**, which will include webinars that dive deep into each stage of this journey, as well as live coaching sessions. You can **join my community** at *stevechamberlain.co.uk/livingonpurpose* to be the first to discover the launch date, and to receive further insights and tools to help you live *on purpose*.

Thank you

Thank you for taking the time to read this book and I hope you've found it to be a valuable resource on your journey. Please don't be fooled into thinking I do everything outlined here perfectly every day... I don't! Just like everyone else, I make mistakes, forget what works and stray from my path, before remembering once more and getting back on track. This is a lifetime's work, so my invitation is to be patient and forgiving of yourself with each and every step. I wish you the very best with your next exciting stage, as you live your life *on purpose*.

ACKNOWLEDGEMENTS

To my parents, John and Carol (I know you're hearing this somewhere, Mum), thank you for being there for me, always. What more could any child ask for?

To Claire, thank you for being there through the darkest days on my journey, when I was well and truly off purpose. I can only imagine how tough it must have been at times. You've shown me it's possible to take risks, follow your heart and fight for what you believe in.

To Jacob and Seren, for teaching me everything there is to know about being present, mindful and playful. It's a privilege to be your Dad.

To Brendan Barns, thank you for taking a punt on a 23-year-old with no events experience and little confidence! You gave me my first break into the world of personal development at London Business Forum, and showed me it's possible to make a dream become reality, with guts and perseverance.

To Elke Edwards and Clare Mitchell – founders of the Ivy House programme – thank you for your radical support and challenge over the past few years. You're doing extraordinary work helping to develop the next generation of leaders, and it's a privilege to play a part in this journey.

To Stephen Wood, Clare Mitchell, Justin and Eleanor Blake, Meg O'Loughlin and Claire for your support editing the book, telling me when things made no sense and, quite frankly, when my writing was a bit crap! Also to Patrick Fogarty for your amazing illustrations and cover design, and Helena Traill for your skill and focus when crafting the layout.

To all my courageous clients, some of whose stories are touched on here and many more that could have been. It's a genuine privilege to work with you – thank you for showing up with such courage and vulnerability.

Finally, to you, the reader. Time is our most precious resource and you have taken the time to engage with this book. Thank you – I hope your investment pays back over a lifetime.

Printed in Germany
by Amazon Distribution
GmbH, Leipzig